W9-CGQ-414

PLACE IN RETURN BOX to remove this checkout from your record.
TO AVOID FINES return on or before date due.

DATE DUE	DATE DUE	DATE DUE
APR 3 0 1995 114	MAR 1 69 2000	
MAR 0 4 1996	APR 2 5 2001 0426 01	
1997	FEB 2 5 2003 APR 2003 2003	
2 9 2 1997	MAR 1 5 8 2006 MAR 2 0 2014	6
MAGIC 2 352 DEC 1 1 1998		
NOV 1 5 1999		

MSU Is An Affirmative Action/Equal Opportunity Institution

c:\circ\datedue.pm3-p.1

Richard B. Sherman *is Associate Professor of History at the College of William and Mary. His numerous articles include "The Harding Administration and the Negro: An Opportunity Lost" and "Republicans and Negroes: The Lessons of Normalcy."*

THE NEGRO
AND THE CITY

edited by

RICHARD B. SHERMAN

PRENTICE-HALL, INC., Englewood Cliffs, N.J.

For Hanni

B40l00l

Contents

THE NEGRO
AND THE CITY

Introduction

Americans have traditionally been of two minds about the city. For some it has beckoned as a place of liberation, an exciting center of economic and intellectual opportunity. Others, however, have seen it only as a place of violence and corruption, a threat to the well-being of the whole society. Booker T. Washington, the most important Negro spokesman at the beginning of the twentieth century, took the latter position. For Negroes, at least, he regarded the city as a danger to be avoided. Their future, he advised, was, like their past, in the rural South.

Washington died in 1915, just as the first of a series of great Negro migrations to the cities of the North and West was getting underway. He would hardly have viewed with favor the tremendous changes that have come about since that time, changes that have resulted in an enormous shift of Negro population in the United States from the South to the North and from the country to the city. This is not to conclude that Washington's position was entirely correct. Like other Americans, Negroes had to seek opportunities where they existed. There simply were not enough in the country, and especially not in the rural South. For the migrants the city beckoned as an escape from poverty, from near-slavery, from violence and from officially sanctioned injustice. The city offered first of all the chance for a new job with high wages. Beyond that was the promise of a good education for their children and, in the North at least, the prospect of decent treatment and even the chance to vote. In short, the city meant hope.

The first great Negro migrations to the city in the twentieth century

I

took place during the period of the First World War and the early 1920s. These were followed by an even larger movement that began during the Second World War and continued through the 1960s. As a result, the nature of America's racial problems has been drastically altered. What was once preeminently a southern matter has become an issue of first importance for the whole country. Before the great migrations, nearly 90 per cent of the blacks in the United States lived in the South, mostly in rural areas. Today they are spread throughout the country and are heavily concentrated in the central parts of the cities, North and South. Over two-thirds of the residents of Washington, D.C., are now Negroes. Negroes make up nearly half the population of Newark, more than 40 per cent in Atlanta, New Orleans, and Memphis, and about a third in Baltimore, Cleveland, Detroit, and Philadelphia. There are also huge concentrations of blacks in Chicago, New York, and Los Angeles. In all of these cities, as well as in many smaller ones, the Negro proportion of the population has been steadily increasing. No important city today is without its serious racial problems. The black ghetto has replaced the black belt as the symbol of the American dilemma.

This book is concerned with the experience of black Americans—their hopes, their problems, their reactions—in the city since the latter part of the nineteenth century. It also deals to some extent with the response of white America to the Negro urbanization. While this process has been primarily a product of twentieth-century migration, some Negroes lived in the cities of the North and South long before that time. A few selections deal with this older group. Most of the material, however, is from the period of the First World War to the present and is primarily concerned with cities in the North. Of necessity, the book is highly selective and makes no pretense of covering all aspects of Negro urban life. Meaningful excerpts on some subjects could not be included within reasonable space limitations. For other topics, such as urban violence or the black protest movements, the material is so abundant that some interesting examples had to be omitted. But the selections do illustrate the principal issues connected with the urbanization of American Negroes. And they may provide the basis for a better understanding of racial problems in the city.

Unfortunately, this book must deal to a large degree with problems, crises, and disorders, for these have become an inescapable element of twentieth-century urban life in the United States. Thus, in part, the selections illustrate the extent to which the highest hopes of the migrants were frustrated in the city. After describing the migrations the selections turn to the major immediate challenges faced by the black newcomers: the search for a place to live, for a job, and for decent schools. Certain similarities can be seen in all three cases. The initial optimism of the migrants was checked by harsh realities; the federal government eventually became involved in attempts to alleviate difficulties; and the problems, far from being readily resolved, successfully resisted any simple solution. The urban crisis is revealed in its most horrible and elemental form in the violent racial conflicts that have disgraced so many American cities since 1900. A few selections try to put these in broader perspective. But the city meant much more than crisis, for from it have come many positive contributions to Negro life, from the Harlem Renaissance of the 1920s to more recent lessons in the constructive use of economic and political power. These, too, are illustrated in this book as part of the urban experience of black Americans.

In recent years the tendency to write about American cities in terms of crisis and disaster has become almost overwhelming. The numerous difficulties are all too apparent, although they are, of course, only partly related to the great influx and growth of Negro population. Certainly, however, there is enough evidence on the negative side to vindicate some of Booker T. Washington's worst fears. But there is another aspect to the story. For all the deficiencies of the city schools, for example, Negroes did find educational opportunities that were wholly unavailable to them in the rural South. Similarly, employment prospects were far more diverse in the city than in the country. Beyond that, urban life broadened the social and intellectual horizons of Negroes and helped make them more conscious of their identity and strength as a group. Hence from the city emerged an expanded cultural life, a new racial pride, and new racial leaders. It would be foolish to minimize the seriousness of the contemporary urban crisis. Still, in reflecting on the experience of Negroes it may be useful to recall the traditional ambivalence Americans have felt about the city and to recognize that it has presented opportunities for good as well as evil, for hope as well as disaster.

I To the City

In 1900 nearly 90 per cent of the Negroes in the United States lived in the South. Fewer than one out of four were classified as urban residents. Although a steady stream of blacks had moved away from the southern countryside since the Civil War, the total number was too small to alter very significantly the general population distribution. Thus the 90.6 per cent of the Negro population living in the South in 1870 fell to only 89.7 in 1900. Migration picked up during the 1890s and especially after the turn of the century, but it was not until the First World War that it suddenly reached flood proportions. A second great wave followed during the first half of the 1920s. The impact of this movement on some northern cities was dramatic. Detroit's Negro population jumped from 4,111 in 1900 to 120,066 in 1930; Chicago's increased from 30,150 to 233,903; New York's from 60,666 to 327,706. The creation of Harlem as the Negro metropolis of the United States was a product of this period.

Migration slackened during the depression years of the 1930s, but a new and greater flow began during the Second World War, and this movement only recently has shown signs of abating. By the latter part of the 1960s the distribution of the Negro population was vastly different from what it had been at the beginning of the century. About half of the country's blacks now lived outside of the South, and about three out of four in a city. Even in Dixie nearly 60 per cent, compared to a mere 17.2 per cent in 1900, were classified as urban, while in the North and West the figure was over 95 per cent.

The first selections in this book are concerned with these great migrations and the transformation of the city that was brought about by them.

5

1   THE MIGRATION OF 1916–1918

*Until the First World War the movement of Negroes from the South to
the North, which had been going on fairly steadily since the 1860s,
attracted relatively little attention. It was a different matter in 1916–1918,
when nearly half a million blacks descended upon the northern cities.
There were several reasons for this sudden outpouring, the most
important being economic. The decline in European immigration,
coupled with the demands of the war industries, created a serious labor
shortage. Thus northern employers turned to the South to recruit new
workers. The migration was also caused by many problems in the
South, such as crop failures, low wages, brutality, and injustice. Many
Negroes believed that in the North they would find something close to
the Promised Land. Large numbers of them headed for Chicago, where
Robert S. Abbott's Chicago Defender, the most influential Negro
newspaper of the period, did its best to keep alive that hope. This
selection illustrates some of the techniques used by the Defender.*

From the Chicago Commission on Race Relations, The Negro in
Chicago: A Study of Race Relations and a Race Riot (*Chicago:
The University of Chicago Press, 1922*), *pp. 87–90, 92.*

Chicago was the logical destination of Negroes from Mississippi,
Arkansas, Alabama, Louisiana, and Texas, because of the more direct
railway lines, the way in which the city had become known in these
sections through its two great mail-order houses, the Stock Yards, and the
packing-plants with their numerous storage houses scattered in various
towns and cities of the South. It was rumored in these sections that the
Stock Yards needed 50,000 men; it was said that temporary housing was
being provided by these hard-pressed industries. Many Negroes came to
the city on free transportation, but by far the greater numbers paid their
own fare. Club rates offered by the railroads brought the fare within reach
of many who ordinarily could not have brought their families or even
come themselves. The organization into clubs composed of from ten to
fifty persons from the same community had the effect, on the one hand,
of adding the stimulus of intimate persuasion to the movement, and, on
the other hand, of concentrating solid groups in congested spots in
Chicago.

A study of certain Negro periodicals shows a powerful influence on southern Negroes already in a state of unsettlement over news of the "opening up of the North."

The *Chicago Defender* became a "herald of glad tidings" to southern Negroes. Several cities attempted to prevent its circulation among their Negro population and confiscated the street- and store-sales supplies as fast as they came. Negroes then relied upon subscription copies delivered through the mails. There are reports of the clandestine circulation of copies of the paper in bundles of merchandise. A correspondent of the *Defender* wrote: "White people are paying more attention to the race in order to keep them in the South, but the *Chicago Defender* has emblazoned upon their minds 'Bound for the Promised Land.' "

In Gulfport, Mississippi, it was stated, a man was regarded "intelligent" if he read the *Defender*, and in Laurel, Mississippi, it was said that old men who had never known how to read, bought the paper simply because it was regarded as precious.

Articles and headlines carrying this special appeal which appeared in the *Defender* are quoted:

Why Should the Negro Stay in the South?
West Indians Live North

It is true the South is nice and warm, and may I add, so is China, and we find Chinamen living in the North, East, and West. So is Japan, but the Japanese are living everywhere.

School Boards Bad

While in Arkansas a member of the school board in one of the cities of that state (and it is said it is the rule throughout the South that a Race woman teacher to hold her school must be on friendly terms with some one of them) lived openly with a Race woman, and the entire Race, men and women, were afraid to protest or stop their children from going to school, because this school board member would get up a mob and run them out of the state. They must stomach this treatment.

Frozen Death Better

To die from the bite of frost is far more glorious than that of the mob. I beg of you, my brothers, to leave that benighted land. You are free men. Show the world that you will not let false leaders lead you. Your neck has been in the yoke. Will you continue to keep it there because some "white folks Nigger" wants you to? Leave to all quarters of the globe. Get out of the South. Your being there in the numbers you are gives the southern politician too strong a hold on your progress.

Turn Deaf Ear

Turn a deaf ear to everybody. You see they are not lifting their laws to help you, are they? Have they stopped their Jim Crow cars? Can you buy a Pullman sleeper where you wish? Will they give you a square deal in court yet? When a girl is sent to prison, she becomes the mistress of the guards and others in authority, and women prisoners are put on the streets to work, something they don't do to a white woman. And your leaders will tell you the South is the best place for you. Turn a deaf ear to the scoundrel, and let him stay. Above all, see to it that that jumping-jack preacher is left at the South, for he means you no good here at the North. . . .

News articles in the *Defender* kept alive the enthusiasm and fervor of the exodus:

Leaving for the North

Tampa, Fla., Jan. 19. J. T. King, supposed to be a race leader, is using his wits to get on the good side of the white people by calling a meeting to urge our people not to migrate North. King has been termed a "good nigger" by his pernicious activity on the emigration question. Reports have been received here that all who have gone North are at work and pleased with the splendid conditions in the North. It is known here that in the North there is a scarcity of labor, mills and factories are open to them. People are not paying any attention to King and are packing and ready to travel North to the "promised land." . . .

Thomas Likes the North

J. H. Thomas, Birmingham, Ala., Brownsville Colony, has been here several weeks and is very much pleased with the North. He is working at the Pullman shops, making twice as much as he did at home. Mr. Thomas says the "exodus" will be greater later on in the year, that he did not find four feet of snow or freeze to death. He lives at 346 East Thirty-fifth St.

Leaving for the East

Huntsville, Ala., Jan. 19. Fifteen families, all members of the Race, left here today for Pittsburgh, Pa., where they will take positions as butlers and maids, getting sixty to seventy-five dollars per month, against fifteen and twenty paid here. Most of them claim that they have letters from their friends who went early and made good, saying that there was plenty of work, and this field of labor is short, owing to the vast amount of men having gone to Europe and not returned.

They're Leaving Memphis in Droves

Some are coming on the passenger,
Some are coming on the freight,
Others will be found walking,
For none have time to wait.

Other headlines read: "Thousands Leave Memphis"; "Still Planning to Come North"; "Northbound Their Cry." These articles are especially interesting for the impelling power of the suggestion of a great mass movement.

The idea that the South is a bad place, unfit for the habitation of Negroes, was "played up" and emphasized by the *Defender*. Conditions most distasteful to Negroes were given first prominence. In this it had a clear field, for the local southern Negro papers dared not make such unrestrained utterances. Articles of this type appeared:

Exodus to Start

Forest City, Ark., Feb. 16. David B. Smith (white) is on trial for life for the brutal murder of a member of the Race, W. H. Winford, who refused to be whipped like others. This white man had the habit of making his "slave" submit to this sort of punishment and when Winford refused to stand for it, he was whipped to death with a "black snake" whip. The trial of Smith is attracting very little attention. As a matter of fact, the white people here think nothing of it as the dead man is a "nigger."

This very act, coupled with other recent outrages that have been heaped upon our people, are causing thousands to leave, not waiting for the great spring movement in May.

• • •

It is probably no exaggeration to say that the *Defender's* policy prompted thousands of restless Negroes to venture North, where they were assured of its protection and championship of their cause. Many migrants in Chicago attribute their presence in the North to the *Defender's* encouraging pictures of relief from conditions at home with which they became increasingly dissatisfied as they read.

2 LETTERS OF NEGRO MIGRANTS

The conditions that prompted many Negroes to leave the South and their hopes for life in the North are well illustrated by some of the letters written by the migrants of 1916–1918. These letters also suggest the influence of the Chicago Defender, as well as correspondence with friends and relatives back in the South, on continuing migration. They are taken from a collection assembled by Emmett J. Scott, the former

secretary to Booker T. Washington, who served as a special advisor to
the federal government on Negro matters during the First World War.

From "Letters of Negro Migrants of 1916–1918," Journal of Negro
History 4, No. 3 (July, 1919): 291, 304, 338–39; "Additional
Letters of Negro Migrants of 1916–1918," ibid., 4, No. 4 (October,
1919): 435, 457–58, 461–62, 465. Reprinted by permission of
The Association for the Study of Negro Life and History.

DALLAS, TEX.,
April 23, 1917.

Dear Sir: Having been informed through the Chicago Defender paper
that I can secure information from you. I am a constant reader of the
Defender and am contemplating on leaving here for some point north.
Having your city in view I thought to inquire of you about conditions for
work, housing, wages and everything necessary. I am now employed as a
laborer in a structural shop, have worked for the firm five years.

I stored cars for Armour packing co. 3 years, I also claims to know
something about candy making, am handy at most anything for an honest
living. I am 31 yrs. old have a very industrious wife, no children. If
chances are available for work of any kind let me know. Any information
you can give me will be highly appreciated. . . .

LEXINGTON, MISS., May 12–17.

My dear Mr. H——: I am writing to you for some information and
assistance if you can give it.

I am a young man and am disable, in a very great degree, to do hard
manual labor. I was educated at Alcorn College and have been teaching
a few years: but ah: me the Superintendent under whom we poor colored
teachers have to teach cares less for a colored man than he does for the
vilest beast. I am compelled to teach 150 children without any assistance
and receives only $27.00 a month, the white with 30 get $100.

I am so sick I am so tired of such conditions that I sometime think that
life for me is not worth while and most eminently believe with Patrick
Henry "Give me liberty or give me death." If I was a strong able bodied
man I would have gone from here long ago, but this handicaps me and,
I must make inquiries before I leap.

Mr. H——, do you think you can assist me to a position I am good at
stenography typewriting and bookkeeping or any kind of work not to
rough or heavy. I am 4 feet 6 in high and weigh 105 pounds.

I will gladly give any other information you may desire and will
greatly appreciate any assistance you may render me.

SHERMAN, GA., Nov. 28, 1916.

Dear sir: This letter comes to ask for all infirmations concern-employment in your conection in the warmest climate. Now I am in a family of (11) eleven more or less boys and girls (men and women) mixed sizes who want to go north as soon as arrangements can be made and employment given places for shelter an so en (etc) now this are farming people they were raised on the farm and are good farm hands I of course have some experence and qualefication as a coman school teacher and hotel waiter and along few other lines.

I wish you would write me at your first chance and tell me if you can give us employment at what time and about what wages will you pay and what kind of arrangement can be made for our shelter. Tell me when can you best use us now or later.

Will you send us tickets if so on what terms and at what price what is the cost per head and by what route should we come. We are Negroes and try to show ourselves worthy of all we may get from any friendly source we endeavor to be true to all good causes, if you can we thank you to help us to come north as soon as you can. . . .

GRANVILLE, MISS., May 16, 1917.

Dear Sir: This letter is a letter of information of which you will find stamp envelop for reply. I want to come north some time soon but I do not want to leve here looking for a job wher I would be in dorse all winter. Now the work I am doing here is running a gauge edger in a saw mill. I know all about the grading of lumber. I have abeen working in lumber about 25 or 27 years My wedges here is $3.00 a day 11 hours a day. I want to come north where I can educate my 3 little children also my wife. Now if you cannot fit me up at what I am doing down here I can learn anything any one els can. also there is a great deal of good women cooks here would leave any time all they want is to know where to go and some way to go. please write me at once just how I can get my people where they can get something for their work. there are women here cookeing for $1.50 and $2.00 a week. I would like to live in Chicago or Ohio or Phila-delphia. Tell Mr Abbott that our pepel are tole that they can not get anything to do up there and they are being snatched off the trains here in Greenville and a rested but in spite of all this, they are leaving every day and every night 100 or more is expecting to leave this week. Let me here from you at once. . . .

CHICAGO, ILLINOIS.

My dear Sister: I was agreeably surprised to hear from you and to hear from home. I am well and thankful to say I am doing well. The weather and everything else was a surprise to me when I came. I got here in time to attend one of the greatest revivals in the history of my life—over 500 people joined the church. We had a Holy Ghost shower. You know I like to have run wild. It was snowing some nights and if you didnt hurry you could not get standing room. Please remember me kindly to any who ask of me. The people are rushing here by the thousands and I know if you come and rent a big house you can get all the roomers you want. You write me exactly when you are coming. I am not keeping house yet I am living with my brother and his wife. My sone is in California but will be home soon. He spends his winter in California. I can get a nice place for you to stop until you can look around and see what you want. I am quite busy. I work in Swifts packing Co. in the sausage department. My daughter and I work for the same company—We get $1.50 a day and we pack so many sausages we dont have much time to play but it is a matter of a dollar with me and I feel that God made the path and I am walking therein.

Tell your husband work is plentiful here and he wont have to loaf if he want to work. I know unless old man A—— changed it was awful with his sould and G—— also.

Well I am always glad to hear from my friends and if I can do anything to assist any of them to better their condition. please remember me to Mr. C—— and his family I will write them all as soon as I can. Well I guess I have said about enough. I will be delighted to look into your face once more in life. Pray for me for I am heaven bound. I have made too many rounds to slip now. I know you will pray for prayer is the life of any sensible man or woman. Well goodbye from your sister in Christ

P. S. My brother moved the week after I came. When you fully decide to come write me and let me know what day you expect to leave and over what road and if I dont meet you I will have some one ther to meet you and look after you. I will send you a paper as soon as one come along they send out extras two and three times a day.

PHILADELPHIA, PA., Oct. 7, 1917.

Dear Sir: I take this method of thanking you for yours early responding and the glorious effect of the treatment. Oh. I do feel so fine. Dr. the treatment reach me almost ready to move I am now housekeeping again I like it so much better than rooming. Well Dr. with the aid of God I am making very good I make $75 per month. I am carrying enough insurance to pay me $20 per week if I am not able to be on duty. I don't have to work hard. dont have to mister every little white boy comes along I havent heard a white man call a colored a nigger you no now—since I been in the state of Pa. I can ride in the electric street and steam cars any where I get a seat. I dont care to mix with white what I mean I am not crazy about being with white folks, but if I have to pay the same fare I have learn to want the same acomidation. and if you are first in a place here shoping you dont have to wait until the white folks get thro tradeing yet amid all this I shall ever love the good old South and I am praying that God may give every well wisher a chance to be a man regardless of his color, and if my going to the front would bring about such conditions I am ready any day—well Dr. I dont want to worry you but read between lines; and maybe you can see a little sense in my weak statement the kids are in school every day I have only two and I guess that all. Dr. when you find time I would be delighted to have a word from the good old home state. Wife join me in sending love you and yours.

I am your friend and patient.

AKRON, OHIO, May 21, 1917.

Dear Friend: I am well and hop you are well. I am getting along fine I have not been sick since I left home I have not lost but $2\frac{1}{2}$ day I work like a man. I am making good. I never liked a place like I do here except home. Their is no place like home How is the church getting along. You cant hardly get a house to live in I am wide awake on my financial plans. I have rent me a place for boarders I have 15 sleprs I began one week ago and be shure to send me my letter of dismission By Return mail. I am going into some kind of business here by the first of Sept. Are you farming. Rasion is mighty high up here. the people are coming from the south every week the colored people are making good they are the best workers. I have made a great many white friends. The Baptist Church is over crowded with Baptist from Ala & Ga. 10 and 12 join every sunday. He is planning to build a fine brick church. He takes up 50 and 60 dollars each sunday he is a wel to do preacher. I am going to send you a check for my salary in a few weeks. It cose me $100 to buy furniture. Write me.

3 THE CITY TRANSFORMED

During the 1930s the flow of Negroes from the South to the North dropped to less than half of what it had been in the previous decade. The next great migration began during World War II, when once again the demand for labor opened up new economic opportunities. The outpouring from the South was greatest during the 1940s, but, with some yearly variations, the volume continued high throughout the 1950s and 1960s. The main outline of this migration and its effect on American cities is cogently stated in this selection.

From *the* Report of the National Advisory Commission on Civil
Disorders (*Washington, D.C.: U.S. Government Printing Office,
1968*), *pp. 117–20. Tables and footnotes have been omitted.*

IMPORTANT CHARACTERISTICS OF THIS MIGRATION

It is useful to recall that even the latest scale of Negro migration is
relatively small when compared to the earlier waves of European immigrants. A total of 8.8 million immigrants entered the United States
between 1901 and 1911, and another 5.7 million arrived during the
following decade. Even during the years from 1960 through 1966, the
1.8 million immigrants from abroad were almost three times the 613,000
Negroes who departed the South. In these same 6 years, California alone
gained over 1.5 million new residents from internal shifts of American
population.

Three major routes of Negro migration from the South have developed.
One runs north along the Atlantic Seaboard toward Boston, another
north from Mississippi toward Chicago, and the third west from Texas
and Louisiana toward California. Between 1955 and 1960, 50 per cent of
the nonwhite migrants to the New York metropolitan area came from
North Carolina, South Carolina, Virginia, Georgia, and Alabama; North
Carolina alone supplied 20 per cent of all New York's nonwhite immigrants. During the same period, almost 60 per cent of the nonwhite
migrants to Chicago came from Mississippi, Tennessee, Arkansas, Alabama, and Louisiana; Mississippi accounted for almost one-third. During
these years, three-fourths of the nonwhite migrants to Los Angeles came
from Texas, Louisiana, Mississippi, Arkansas, and Alabama.

The flow of Negroes from the South has caused the Negro population
to grow more rapidly in the North and West. . . .

As a result, although a much higher proportion of Negroes still reside
in the South, the distribution of Negroes throughout the United States is
beginning to approximate that of whites. . . .

Negroes in the North and West are now so numerous that natural
increase rather than migration provides the greater part of Negro population gains there. And even though Negro migration has continued at a
high level, it comprises a constantly declining proportion of Negro growth
in these regions. . . .

In other words, we have reached the point where the Negro populations of the North and West will continue to expand significantly even
if migration from the South drops substantially. . . .

WHERE NEGRO URBANIZATION HAS OCCURRED

Statistically, the Negro population in America has become more urbanized, and more metropolitan, than the white population. According to Census Bureau estimates, almost 70 per cent of all Negroes in 1966 lived in metropolitan areas, compared to 64 per cent of all whites. In the South, more than half the Negro population now lives in cities. Rural Negroes outnumber urban Negroes in only four states: Arkansas, Mississippi, North Carolina, and South Carolina.

Basic data concerning Negro urbanization trends . . . indicate that:

Almost all Negro population growth is occurring within metropolitan areas, primarily within central cities. From 1950 to 1966, the U.S. Negro population rose 6.5 million. Over 98 percent of that increase took place in metropolitan areas—86 percent within central cities, 12 percent in the urban fringe.

The vast majority of white population growth is occurring in suburban portions of metropolitan areas. From 1950 to 1966, 77.8 percent of the white population increase of 35.6 million took place in the suburbs. Central cities received only 2.5 percent of this total white increase. Since 1960, white central-city population has actually declined by 1.3 million.

As a result, central cities are steadily becoming more heavily Negro, while the urban fringes around them remain almost entirely white. The proportion of Negroes in all central cities rose steadily from 12 percent in 1950, to 17 percent in 1966, to 20 percent in 1966. Meanwhile, metropolitan areas outside of central cities remained 95 percent white from 1950 to 1960 and became 96 percent white by 1966.

The Negro population is growing faster, both absolutely and relatively, in the larger metropolitan areas than in the smaller ones. From 1950 to 1966, the proportion of nonwhites in the central cities of metropolitan areas with 1 million or more persons doubled, reaching 26 percent, as compared with 20 percent in the central cities of metropolitan areas containing from 250,000 to 1 million persons and 12 percent in the central cities of metropolitan areas containing under 250,000 persons.

The 12 largest central cities—New York, Chicago, Los Angeles, Philadelphia, Detroit, Baltimore, Houston, Cleveland, Washington, D.C., St. Louis, Milwaukee, and San Francisco—now contain over two-thirds of the Negro population outside the South and almost one-third of the total in the United States. All these cities have experienced rapid increases in Negro population since 1950. In six—Chicago, Detroit, Cleveland, St. Louis, Milwaukee, and San Francisco—the proportion of Negroes at least doubled. In two others—New York and Los Angeles—it probably doubled. In 1968, seven of these cities are over 30 percent Negro, and one, Washington, D.C., is two-thirds Negro.

FACTORS CAUSING RESIDENTIAL SEGREGATION IN METROPOLITAN AREAS

The early pattern of Negro settlement within each metropolitan area followed that of immigrant groups. Migrants converged on the older sections of the central city because the lowest cost housing was located there, friends and relatives were likely to be living there, and the older neighborhoods then often had good public transportation.

But the later phases of Negro settlement and expansion in metropolitan areas diverge sharply from those typical of white immigrants. As the whites were absorbed by the larger society, many left their predominantly ethnic neighborhoods and moved to outlying areas to obtain newer housing and better schools. Some scattered randomly over the suburban area. Others established new ethnic clusters in the suburbs, but even these rarely contained solely members of a single ethnic group. As a result, most middle-class neighborhoods—both in the suburbs and within central cities—have no distinctive ethnic character, except that they are white.

Nowhere has the expansion of America's urban Negro population followed this pattern of dispersal. Thousands of Negro families have attained incomes, living standards, and cultural levels matching or surpassing those of whites who have "upgraded" themselves from distinctly ethnic neighborhoods. Yet most Negro families have remained within predominantly Negro neighborhoods, primarily because they have been effectively excluded from white residential areas.

Their exclusion has been accomplished through various discriminatory practices, some obvious and overt, others subtle and hidden. Deliberate efforts are sometimes made to discourage Negro families from purchasing or renting homes in all-white neighborhoods. Intimidation and threats of violence have ranged from throwing garbage on lawns and making threatening phone calls to burning crosses in yards and even dynamiting property. More often, real estate agents simply refuse to show homes to Negro buyers.

Many middle-class Negro families, therefore, cease looking for homes beyond all-Negro areas or nearby "changing" neighborhoods. For them, trying to move into all-white neighborhoods is not worth the psychological efforts and costs required.

Another form of discrimination just as significant is white withdrawal from, or refusal to enter, neighborhoods where large numbers of Negroes are moving or already residing. Normal population turnover causes about 20 per cent of the residents of average U.S. neighborhoods to move out every year because of income changes, job transfers, shifts in life-cycle position or deaths. This normal turnover rate is even higher in apartment areas. The refusal of whites to move into changing areas when vacancies occur there from normal turnover means that most of these vacancies are eventually occupied by Negroes. An inexorable shift toward heavy Negro occupancy results.

Once this happens, the remaining whites seek to leave, thus confirming the existing belief among whites that complete transformation of a neighborhood is inevitable once Negroes begin to enter. Since the belief itself is one of the major causes of the transformation, it becomes a self-fulfilling prophecy which inhibits the development of racially integrated neighborhoods.

As a result, Negro settlements expand almost entirely through "massive racial transition" at the edges of existing all-Negro neighborhoods, rather than by a gradual dispersion of population throughout the metropolitan area.

Two points are particularly important:

> "Massive transition" requires no panic or flight by the original white residents of a neighborhood into which Negroes begin moving. All it requires is the failure or refusal of other whites to fill the vacancies resulting from normal turnover.
>
> Thus, efforts to stop massive transition by persuading present white residents to remain will ultimately fail unless whites outside the neighborhood can be persuaded to move in.

It is obviously true that some residential separation of whites and Negroes would occur even without discriminatory practices by whites. This would result from the desires of some Negroes to live in predominantly Negro neighborhoods and from differences in meaningful social variables, such as income and educational levels. But these factors alone would not lead to the almost complete segregation of whites and Negroes which has developed in our metropolitan areas.

THE EXODUS OF WHITES FROM CENTRAL CITIES

The process of racial transition in central-city neighborhoods has been only one factor among many others causing millions of whites to move out of central cities as the Negro populations there expanded. More basic perhaps have been the rising mobility and affluence of middle-class families and the more attractive living conditions—particularly better schools—in the suburbs.

Whatever the reason, the result is clear. In 1950, 45.5 million whites lived in central cities. If this population had grown from 1950 to 1960 at the same rate as the Nation's white population as a whole, it would have increased by 8 million. It actually rose only 2.2 million, indicating an outflow of 5.8 million.

From 1960 to 1966, the white outflow appears to have been even more rapid. White population of central cities declined 1.3 million instead of rising 3.6 million—as it would if it had grown at the same rate as the entire white population. In theory, therefore, 4.9 million whites left central cities during these 6 years.

Statistics for all central cities as a group understate the relationship between Negro population growth and white outflow in individual central cities. The fact is, many cities with relatively few Negroes experienced rapid white-population growth, thereby obscuring the size of white out-migration that took place in cities having large increases in Negro population. For example, from 1950 to 1960, the 10 largest cities in the United States had a total Negro population increase of 1.6 million, or 55 per cent, while the white population there declined 1.4 million. If the two cities where the white population increased (Los Angeles and Houston) are excluded, the nonwhite population in the remaining eight cities rose 1.4 million, whereas their white population declined 2.1 million. If the white population in these cities had increased at only half the rate of the white population in the United States as a whole from 1950 to 1960, it would have risen by 1.4 million. Thus, these eight cities actually experienced a white outmigration of at least 3.5 million, while gaining 1.4 million nonwhites.

THE EXTENT OF RESIDENTIAL SEGREGATION

The rapid expansion of all-Negro residential areas and large-scale white withdrawal have continued a pattern of residential segregation that has existed in American cities for decades. . . .

Residential segregation is generally more prevalent with respect to Negroes than for any other minority group, including Puerto Ricans, Orientals, and Mexican-Americans. Moreover, it varies little between central city and suburb. This nearly universal pattern cannot be explained in terms of economic discrimination against all low-income groups. Analysis of 15 representative cities indicates that white upper- and middle-income households are far more segregated from Negro upper- and middle-income households than from white lower-income households.

In summary, the concentration of Negroes in central cities results from a combination of forces. Some of these forces, such as migration and initial settlement patterns in older neighborhoods, are similar to those which affected previous ethnic minorities. Others—particularly discrimination in employment and segregation in housing and schools—are a result of white attitudes based on race and color. These forces continue to shape the future of the central city.

II   A Place To Live

No city was prepared to provide adequate housing on the scale made necessary by the great increase in Negro population. The best opportunity for new migrants to find shelter in the city was in areas already inhabited by Negroes. But the pressure on available housing became overwhelming. The black sections had to expand to meet the needs of the rapidly growing population, and frightened whites tried various methods to contain the Negro population. This section illustrates different aspects of the housing problem, including some of the techniques used to restrict the blacks within limited areas, the physical conditions of some of the housing, and the response of the federal government to the problem.

1 BOOKER T. WASHINGTON
ATTACKS SEGREGATION

In cities of the South and the border states the legislation of residential segregation was attempted as a means of restricting the Negro population. Such devices were seen by many whites as a logical extension of the Jim Crow laws that were being enacted throughout the South since the 1890s. The United States Supreme Court gave a green light to that movement in the case of Plessy v. Ferguson (1896) when it upheld a Louisiana statute requiring railroads to provide separate but equal accommodations for white and Negro passengers. Although Booker T. Washington was not outspoken in his opposition to most forms of racial segregation, in this article, written shortly before his death, he strongly denounced the attempt to maintain residential segregation by law. Two years later, in 1917, the Supreme Court ruled in Buchanan v. Warley that a Louisville, Kentucky, residential segregation ordinance was an unconstitutional interference with property rights in violation of the Fourteenth Amendment. The result was that other methods became more commonly used to achieve much the same end.

From Booker T. Washington, "My View of Segregation Laws,"
The New Republic 5 *(December 4, 1915): 113–14.*

In all of my experience I have never yet found a case where the masses of the people of any given city were interested in the matter of the segregation of white and colored people; that is, there has been no spontaneous demand for segregation ordinances. In certain cities politicians have taken the leadership in introducing such segregation ordinances into city councils, and after making an appeal to racial prejudices have succeeded in securing a backing for ordinances which would segregate the negro people from their white fellow citizens. After such ordinances have been introduced it is always difficult, in the present state of public opinion in the South, to have any considerable body of white people oppose them, because their attitude is likely to be misrepresented as favoring negroes against white people. They are, in the main, afraid of the stigma, "negro-lover."

It is probably useless to discuss the legality of segregation; that is a matter which the courts will finally pass upon. It is reasonably certain, however, that the courts in no section of the country would uphold a case where negroes sought to segregate white citizens. This is the most convincing argument that segregation is regarded as illegal, when viewed on its merits by the whole body of our white citizens.

Personally I have little faith in the doctrine that it is necessary to segregate the whites from the blacks to prevent race mixture. The whites are the dominant race in the South, they control the courts, the industries and the government in all of the cities, counties and states except in those few communities where the negroes, seeking some form of self-government, have established a number of experimental towns or communities.

I have never viewed except with amusement the sentiment that white people who live next to negro populations suffer physically, mentally and morally because of their proximity to colored people. Southern white people who have been brought up in this proximity are not inferior to other white people. The President of the United States was born and reared in the South in close contact with black people. Five members of the present Cabinet were born in the South; and many of them, I am sure, had black "mammies." The Speaker of the House of Representatives is a Southern man, the chairmen of leading committees in both the United States Senate and the Lower House of Congress are Southern men. Throughout the country to-day, people occupying the highest positions not only in the government but in education, industry and science, are persons born in the South in close contact with the negro.

Attempts at legal segregation are unnecessary for the reason that the matter of residence is one which naturally settles itself. Both colored and whites are likely to select a section of the city where they will be surrounded by congenial neighbors. It is unusual to hear of a colored man attempting to live where he is surrounded by white people or where he is not welcome. Where attempts are being made to segregate the races legally, it should be noted that in the matter of business no attempt is made to keep the white man from placing his grocery store, his dry goods store, or other enterprise right in the heart of a negro district. This is another searching test which challenges the good faith of segregationists.

It is true that the negro opposes these attempts to restrain him from residing in certain sections of a city or community. He does this not because he wants to mix with the white man socially, but because he feels that such laws are unnecessary. The negro objects to being segregated because it usually means that he will receive inferior accommodations in return for the taxes he pays. If the negro is segregated, it will probably mean that the sewerage in his part of the city will be inferior; that the streets and sidewalks will be neglected; that the street lighting will be poor; that his section of the city will not be kept in order by the police and other authorities; and that the "undesirables" of other races will be placed near him, thereby making it difficult for him to rear his family in decency. It should always be kept in mind that while the negro may not be directly a large taxpayer, he does pay large taxes indirectly. In the last analysis, all will agree that the man who pays house rent pays large taxes, for the price paid for the rent includes payment of the taxes on the property. . . .

In New Orleans, Atlanta, Birmingham, Memphis—indeed in nearly every large city in the South—I have been in the homes of negroes who live in white neighborhoods, and I have yet to find any race friction; the negro goes about his business, the white man about his. Neither the wives nor the children have the slightest trouble. . . .

Summarizing the matter in the large, segregation is ill-advised because:

1. It is unjust.
2. It invites other unjust measures.
3. It will not be productive of good, because practically every thoughtful negro resents its injustice and doubts its sincerity. Any race adjustment based on injustice finally defeats itself. The Civil War is the best illustration of what results where it is attempted to make wrong right or seem to be right.
4. It is unnecessary.
5. It is inconsistent. The negro is segregated from his white neighbor, but white business men are not prevented from doing business in negro neighborhoods.
6. There has been no case of segregation of negroes in the United States that has not widened the breach between the two races. Wherever a form of segregation exists it will be found that it has been administered in such a way as to embitter the negro and harm more or less the moral fibre of the white man. That the negro does not express this constant sense of wrong is no proof that he does not feel it.

It seems to me that the reasons given above, if carefully considered, should serve to prevent further passage of such segregation ordinances as have been adopted in Norfolk, Richmond, Louisville, Baltimore, and one or two cities in South Carolina.

Finally, as I have said in another place, as white and black learn daily to adjust, in a spirit of justice and fair play, those interests which are individual and racial, and to see and feel the importance of those fundamental interests which are common, so will both races grow and prosper. In the long run no individual and no race can succeed which sets itself at war against the common good, for "in the gain or loss of one race, all the rest have equal claim."

2 NEW YORK PROPERTY OWNERS ADOPT A RESTRICTIVE COVENANT

The decision by the Supreme Court in Buchanan v. Warley *was more significant as an indication of a somewhat more sympathetic attitude toward Negroes than as a means of making decent housing readily available to them. Other techniques could be as effective as city ordinances in limiting the neighborhoods open to Negroes. This selection describes the adoption of a restrictive covenant by a group of New York City property owners. While their attempt to stem the influx of blacks into Harlem was, ultimately, not successful, this device became an important means of keeping Negroes out of many white residential areas.*

From The New York Times, *18 February 1911.* © *1911 by The New York Times Company. Reprinted by permission.*

Another shot in the war which West 136th Street property owners have been waging against the encroachments of what they call the "One Hundred and Thirty-fourth Street Black Belt" was fired yesterday when ninety-one of the 136th Street owners, representing 85 per cent of the property between Lenox and Eighth Avenues, filed in the Register's Office in the Hall of Records a voluminous and many paged covenant, in which they bind themselves not to sell or rent their premises to negroes for the next fifteen years.

The property owners bind themselves "not to allow any part of their premises to be occupied in whole or in part by any negro, mulatto, quadroon, or octoroon of either sex either as a tenant, guest, boarder, or occupant in any other capacity, way or manner." Tenants of each house or flat may not employ more than "one male and one female negro or two negresses," mulattoes, quadroons, or octoroons to "perform the duties ordinarily performed by a household servant." There may be, in short, only one black man servant to each family. Some of the signers of the document are owners of apartment houses. The document doesn't forbid their employing negro elevator boys, but no house may have more negro bellboys, janitors, cleaners, or private servants in it than it has families of whites.

The 91 property owners agree that any one who breaks the covenant will render himself or herself liable to equity proceedings, injunction proceedings and damage suits by the others.

The covenant is legalized by the payment of the customary technical dollar by each of the signers. To prevent the covenant being declared unconstitutional the property owners take care to state they have no desire "to preclude or prevent negroes or citizens of African descent from occupying the premises because of their color or race." . . .

The covenant further states that the damage to property values which already has been done by the negro invasion will take fifteen years to repair, and for this reason the property owners bind themselves, their heirs, their successors, and assigns to hold by the terms of the contract for that period.

"The covenant which we have filed in the Register's office simply means that we are not going to allow outside speculators to force down the value of our property 25 per cent without a fight," said one of the covenanters yesterday. "Our objection is in no sense a slur at the colored race. It is an agreement to defend ourselves against a clever blackmailing scheme which is being worked against self-respecting white property owners in various parts of the town. A certain class of real estate speculators, knowing the depreciation in real estate values which always follows a colored invasion, have been making a practice of buying several houses in a respectable and fairly prosperous white neighborhood.

"These houses the speculators immediately advertise as being available for colored tenants. They stick out signs 'Colored Boarders Wanted.' Sometimes they even go so far as to actually encourage negro tenants of disrepute. They force the respectable white property owners of the neighborhood into accepting one of two alternatives, either one of which is exceedingly profitable to the speculators—to buy at an increased figure the property which the speculators are letting to negroes, or sell their own property to the speculators at a reduced price.

"This is the history of real estate in the various 'black belts' of the city. And it might have been the history of our real estate in West 136th Street. Two or three of the houses in the street changed hands, and signs of 'Colored Boarders Wanted' began to be hung out on these houses. Then a cafe on Lenox Avenue, right around the 136th Street corner, was let to a West Thirty-fifth Street colored saloon keeper, who turned it into a negro dance hall. It was at this time that our Harlem Real Estate Protective Association was organized. . . .

"Between last June and December the covenant was circulated among the property owners along the street and 85 per cent signed it at once. Until the covenant was circulated real estate on West 136th Street had fallen off in value from 10 to 20 per cent; two sales have been made recently of houses on the street at increased figures, the sales being subject to the terms of the covenant."

3   NEGRO HOUSING IN DETROIT IN THE 1920s

In no major northern city did the Negro population expand as rapidly as in Detroit in the decade from the end of the First World War to the 1920s. The result was a dangerous overcrowding in housing that was frequently dilapidated and unsanitary. The ominous heightening of racial tensions that developed as pressure for living space increased prompted the city to undertake a study of its black population in 1926. The following excerpt from the report prepared at that time illustrates some of the worst and some of the best housing then available to Negroes.

From the Detroit Bureau of Governmental Research, Inc., The Negro in Detroit, *prepared for the Mayor's Inter-racial Committee (Detroit, 1926), pp. 1–2, 21–24.*

Housing is one of the most serious problems of the Negro in Detroit. For some years the fluctuating shortage in the number of houses for the population in general has had its greatest effect upon the Negro group. In a study of the housing conditions of Negroes in Detroit prepared in 1919 for the Research Bureau of the Associated Charities Mr. Forrester B. Washington makes the following statement:

> There is not a single vacant house or tenement in the several Negro sections of this city. The majority of Negroes are living under such crowded conditions that three or four families in an apartment is the rule rather than the exception. Seventy-five per cent of the Negro homes have so many lodgers that they are really hotels. Stables, garages and cellars have been converted into homes for Negroes. The pool-rooms and gambling clubs are beginning to charge for the privilege of sleeping on pool-room tables over night.

While this dense overcrowding was to be found during the period immediately after the war when practically all house construction was suspended in the Negro district, overcrowding still exists. It is accounted for by the fact that the rents charged Negroes are so exorbitant that it is usually necessary to "double up" in order to meet the expense. But housing conditions have changed considerably since the 1919 Survey and there are now numbers of vacant apartments and houses open [to] Negroes. This change has been caused in part by the larger subdivision development and house-building programs carried on for the past few years by Detroit realtors and building construction companies. White people living on the borders of Negro districts have moved out to new areas, leaving their former residences open for colored occupancy, and a number of Negro subdivisions have also been opened on the outskirts of the city. While these two factors have modified the housing situation for the Negro, sanitary dwellings at a reasonable rent still are the exceptions, especially in the St. Antoine area. . . .

The following cases are brief word descriptions from the notebook of the Board of Health investigator of conditions found in these blocks.

BLOCK 1

A One-Story Frame House

The general condition of the outside of the house bad; porch falling down, window panes broken, foundation weak. The general condition of the interior: walls broken, floors bad. The plumbing out of order. Five rooms, rent $45. One sink and outside toilet. One room without ventilation. Stove heat. Water under house from leaking pipe in wall. Two roomers paying $6 per week. The landlord refused to make repairs. If repairs are made they will get a $10 increase.

A Dormitory Hotel

A two story brick structure once a bakery. On the second floor 50 beds. Beds very dirty, using dark gray blankets as spreads. Men pay 25¢ per night for sleeping. Beds not changed often. Toilets stopped up, bath in a deplorable condition. In one corner of the dormitory about 35 or 40 dirty mattresses piled up, seemingly from a fire. The floors very dirty, walls bad. Men sleeping in their street clothes. On the first floor a restaurant without license selling soup and fish. Water in the back, flies very bad, no sink, foul air and poor ventilation.

A Two-Story House

Frame material. Side and rear yard in bad condition. Shed in rear. House with 11 rooms, 13 persons of which five were children. Rent $75 per month. Three rooms cannot be used on account of the condition. House on the ground. Water in a cellar about two feet. Paper and plaster is off the walls. The place is infested with bed bugs, roaches and rats. Stove heat. Very poor electric lights. Plumbing bad. . . .

BLOCK 1A

A Two-Family House

Two family house, six rooms each. No bath, one outside toilet. Well in the yard. Stove heat, electricity. General condition of the house bad, roof leaks. Side and rear yard poorly kept. Men work at River Rouge (time required to go to work, two hours and twenty minutes). House could be made very attractive by a few repairs and good housekeeping. Family complain of bad water.

A Six-Room Shanty

Exterior of the house tar paper, interior papered with scrap paper. Rooms partitioned off with portiers and quilts. House heated with a cooking stove in kitchen. Kerosene lamps. Husband a Ford employee earning $35 a week. Buying place on contract. Cost $1400 with $100 down and $13 per month. Wife, laundress, does her laundry work at home earning on the average $10 and $12 a week. Furnishings consisted of piano, dining room suite, three iron beds, kitchen stove and table, and stool chairs. The children's ages ranged from six to fourteen. Mother very ignorant, did not believe in education for children. Family carried no insurance whatever. Belonged to no societies or church. Came to Detroit from rural district of Tennessee. Lived at present address five years.

• • •

Cardoni Apartment

Eight family brick apartment with steam heat. The general interior bad. House formerly rented for $40.00. Rent increased to $60.00 and $65.00. Place taken over by colored in 1923. Apartments need decorating. Plumbing needs repair. Window panes broken. Lawns bad. In the basement apartments home brew and whiskey sold. Most of the apartments have night parties and sell drinks. Occupiers claim that rent is so high they have to do this as a means of helping to pay the rent.

Scotten Avenue Residence

A two story frame building on the west side of Scotten Avenue. The house is about 45 feet from the sidewalk with a front lawn, well-kept and attractively arranged with flowers and shrubbery. The house is newly painted with awnings on front. Flower boxes on the porch. Home consists of eight well ventilated rooms. Interior decorating artistically done. Housekeeping excellent. Plumbing and general repairs good. Home purchased in 1920 for $10,000; down payment, $1500, monthly payments $75.00. Monthly payments have been doubled for the last three years, reducing the principal greatly. Husband died two years ago, leaving widow and three children.

Hartford Avenue Residence

Two story frame house, on west side of Hartford Avenue. Six rooms, toilet, bath, gas and electricity. General condition of interior good. Plumbing good. Hot air heat. Place purchased in 1921, for $4800. Down payment, $1250; monthly payment, $35. Housekeeping is good. The owner is a widow with five children. Sold property in Oklahoma to purchase this home. Mother does day work. House neatly furnished and very clean. Four children in school. Three-car garage. Fine back lawn and side yard.

4 THE FHA SUPPORTS RESIDENTIAL SEGREGATION

Established in 1934, the Federal Housing Administration encouraged home repairs and new construction by insuring loans made by private lending institutions. Its activities, however, often tended to support residential segregation. Robert C. Weaver, who became the first Negro cabinet member in 1966 as Secretary of the Department of Housing and Urban Development, describes such practices in this selection.

From Robert C. Weaver, The Negro Ghetto (New York: Harcourt, Brace and Co., 1948), pp. 217–22. Reprinted by permission of Robert C. Weaver. Footnotes have been omitted.

. . . FHA acceptance and perpetuation of race restrictive covenants and residential segregation prior to the war housing program have been well established. They were effected chiefly through the provisions of the *Underwriting Manual* and the practices of FHA representatives in the field, who are drawn largely from the real estate fraternity and financial institutions. A recent example of the operations of FHA in regard to housing for Negroes is offered by wartime experience in Los Angeles.

During World War II, a local builder was ready to construct priority housing for Negroes in Los Angeles, and a leading bank in the city was prepared to take up the FHA-insured mortgages. When the district real estate operators and some surrounding white owners objected to a project for Negro occupancy in the area, the chief underwriter in the region "reconsidered" the project and came to the conclusion (later proved to be erroneous) that the proposed site was almost completely surrounded by properties affected by race restrictive covenants. He then declared that FHA could not insure the mortgages on homes for Negro occupancy. Even when confronted with evidence, based on the records of the California Title Association, that there were no racial covenants on four sides, he remained adamant and the project was withdrawn from Negro occupancy.

The most damning evidence against FHA during the war housing program was its refusal to approve for insurance the proposed Day Village project in Chester, Pa. That the sponsor was well able technically and financially to carry out such a development was amply illustrated by its successful completion and operation of Day Village just outside Baltimore. The latter project is one of the best planned and constructed private, large-scale developments for Negro occupancy. And, interestingly enough, it is FHA-insured. No doubt this was possible because the Baltimore project is in an established Negro community, surrounded by Negroes on one side and a wide expanse of water on the other three.

When the Sun Shipbuilding and Drydock Co., at Chester, announced in 1942 that it intended to man a new yard entirely with Negroes, a long controversy was started. The whole question whether such a segregated labor policy (which subsequently proved impractical) was desirable caused much heat. Few persons imagined at the time that housing would soon be a much greater headache than the mistaken notion of management that segregation was workable in a tight labor market. Experience solved the matter of separate work crews; time did little to ease the housing situation.

Largely as a result of the promotional activities of NHA, the Joseph P. Day Co., of New York, was interested in constructing war housing for Negroes. Because of the pressing need, it decided to go into Chester. After extensive surveys and planning, the company developed a project and applied for FHA-insurance approval. It was rejected, and Chester, like so many other cities, got little privately financed war housing for Negro occupancy.

The basis of the rejection was the site—one of four considered. The first three were either a part of or adjacent to slum areas already inhabited by Negroes and unacceptable to the builder. Although the local FHA representative agreed with the developer that the fourth site was well-suited to sound planning and as good as could be found in the area, he disapproved it on the ground that there would be difficulties in providing utilities, and that adequate school and transportation facilities were lacking. The contractor maintained that no other site in the city would present fewer problems in relation to these matters and that this was the only possible desirable one. The latter point was supported by the fact that FPHA had already rejected all other available sites in and about the city as unsuitable for public war housing for Negroes. Still, the FHA in Washington upheld the decision of its regional representative.

Either the objections raised by FHA were invalid, or, if they were valid, there could be no war housing in the city. Also, the objections did not actually conflict with minimum FHA standards at the time; they were, at best, objections which could be raised against most projects then currently approved. They were inevitable deficiencies of most sites under wartime conditions of shortage of pipe and wire and general inadequacies in school and transportation facilities. The more the proposed site was compared with other acceptable sites, the more one was forced to conclude that it was far superior in location, topography, and access to existing facilities than most of those on which FHA insured mortgages. The reasons for the rejection were hardly those given. A more plausible explanation is that a large and influential financial institution had invested heavily in a housing project for whites close to the proposed project and was alleged to have put pressure on FHA not to approve housing for Negroes in the area. Regardless of the influence this may have had, it seems clear that FHA rejected the proposed development because it was in a white area. Since there were no suitable sites in Negro areas, this meant that the support of residential segregation by FHA defeated the simultaneous efforts of NHA to encourage private war housing for minorities.

FHA was faced with a dilemma. If there were to be FHA-insured housing for Negroes in northern cities, FHA either had to insure mortgages on Negro homes in sites threatened by blight, or depart from its established practices of rejecting sites for Negro housing outside established Negro neighborhoods. It never relaxed the latter rule; occasionally it departed from established underwriting principles. Detroit offers an example of the latter approach, and the story of the developments there can best be told in the words of FHA:

> One of the most difficult undertakings in the Federal Housing Administration's program of providing housing for minority groups was that involving the insurance of mortgages on approximately 1,000 houses for Negro occupancy in Detroit. The first difficulty was the scarcity of sites in good Negro neighborhoods; secondly, there were no available locations for the development of good Negro subdivisions. As a consequence, the Detroit FHA insuring office elected to set aside an established underwriting principle and accept mortgages for

insurance in strip developments in neighborhoods in which there existed a considerable amount of substandard housing. This is not generally an acceptable practice since experience has shown the value of new dwellings in such neighborhoods rapidly depreciates. The Detroit venture proved simply the reverse. The substandard housing which existed when the new dwellings were constructed has either been improved or demolished; today, the two main neighborhoods in which the new housing was built represent the best Negro small-house developments. The two neighborhoods are, of course, inadequate to meet the demand of Detroit's steadily expanding Negro population, now estimated at about a quarter of a million. They are in widely separated sections of the metropolitan area of Detroit, one just beyond the city limits in the town of Ecorse and the other in the so-called Eight Mile Road section.

The Carver Addition just outside Columbus is an example of an FHA solution to this vexing problem. In this instance FHA insured a project providing 146 single-family homes for Negro veterans and their families. "The new subdivision is located entirely within Hanford Village which has been an incorporated Negro community for nearly 45 years, with its own mayor and council and municipal services. Built in accordance with suggestions of the FHA office, it is convenient to schools, churches, and other necessary community services, with all improvements measuring up to FHA standards." While Carver Addition served to solve the shelter needs of less than 150 Negro families, it provided no formula for meeting similar needs of thousands of others since it did not come to grips with the basic need for opening more living space for colored people in the Columbus area.

In Detroit, Columbus, Chicago, and a score of other cities in the North, pressure from Washington and mounting needs in the locality led local FHA representatives to press for private war housing available to Negroes. In instances in the North where results were obtained, they were possible because an existing area of Negro occupancy was surrounded by vacant land, as in Chicago and Columbus, or because FHA standards were lowered, as in Detroit. In most instances, local FHA offices were not interested in promoting housing for colored occupancy. On the West Coast, for example, this was most pronounced in the Bay Area in and around San Francisco. In several cities in that section private builders were ready to go ahead with war housing for Negro occupants, but the local FHA offices either discouraged such activity during the early war years or remained cool toward proposed plans. In most sections of the Middle West the same situation existed. From conversations with certain FHA officers in the area, it was clear that they actually were opposed to housing for Negroes. Insofar as many of them devoted any attention to the matter, they did so wholly because the racial designation of priorities required them to.

5 THE IMPACT OF THE GHETTO IN THE 1960s

In the case of Shelley v. Kraemer *(1948) the United States Supreme Court took an important step in the direction of freeing Negroes from some of the legal restrictions imposed on them in acquiring and occupying housing. Although it did not hold that restrictive covenants between private individuals violated the Constitution, it did find that the enforcement of such agreements by the state courts was a denial of the equal protection of the laws. However, such constitutional protections extended by an increasingly sympathetic Supreme Court did little to alter the day-to-day realities of the city slum. Dr. Kenneth B. Clark, a professor of social psychology at the City College of New York, has lived much of his life in Harlem and is one of the most perceptive critics of ghetto life. In this selection he discusses the impact of the Harlem slums on the Negro residents.*

From Kenneth B. Clark, Dark Ghetto: Dilemmas of Social Power *(New York: Harper & Row, 1965), pp. 30–34. Copyright © 1965 by Kenneth B. Clark. Reprinted by permission of Harper & Row, Publishers, and Victor Gollancz, Ltd. Footnotes have been omitted.*

Another important aspect of the social dynamics of the Northern urban ghettos is the fact that all are crowded and poor; Harlem houses 232,792 people within its three and one half square miles, a valley between Morningside and Washington Heights and the Harlem River. There are more than 100 people per acre. Ninety per cent of the 87,369 residential buildings are more than thirty-three years old, and nearly half were built before 1900. Private developers have not thought Harlem a good investment: Few of the newer buildings were sponsored by private money, and almost all of those buildings erected since 1929 are post-World War II public housing developments, where a fifth of the population lives.

The condition of all but the newest buildings is poor. Eleven per cent are classified as dilapidated by the 1960 census; that is, they do "not provide safe and adequate shelter," and thirty-three per cent are deteriorating (i.e., "need more repair than would be provided in the course of regular maintenance"). There are more people in fewer rooms than elsewhere in the city. Yet the rents and profits from Harlem are often high, as many landlords deliberately crowd more people into buildings in slum areas, knowing that the poor have few alternatives. The rent per room is often higher in Harlem than for better-equipped buildings downtown. Slum landlords, ready enough when the rent is due, are hard to find when repairs are demanded. Even the city cannot seem to find some of them, and when they go to trial for neglect, they are usually given modest and lenient sentences—compared to the sentences of Harlem teen-agers who defy the law. Cruel in the extreme is the landlord who, like the store owner who charges Negroes more for shoddy merchandise, exploits the powerlessness of the poor. For the poor are not only poor but unprotected and do not know how to seek redress. One is reminded of the Biblical admonition: "For whosoever hath, to him shall be given, and he shall have more abundance: but whosoever hath not, from him shall be taken away even that he hath."

The effects of unsafe, deteriorating, and overcrowded housing upon physical health are well documented and understood. The multiple use of toilet and water facilities, inadequate heating and ventilation, and crowded sleeping quarters increase the rate of acute respiratory infections and infectious childhood diseases. Poor facilities for the storage of food and inadequate washing facilities cause enteritis and skin and digestive disease. Crowded, poorly equipped kitchens, poor electrical connections, and badly lighted and unstable stairs increase the rate of home accidents and fires. Nor is the street any safer. Harlem's fourteen parks, playgrounds, and recreational areas are inadequate and ugly, and many of the children play in the streets where heavy truck traffic flows through the community all day. Far more children and young adults are killed by cars in Harlem than in the rest of the city (6.9 per 100,000 population compared to 4.2 per 100,000 for New York City as a whole).

The physical health of the residents of the ghetto is as impaired as one would expect based on knowledge of its housing conditions. The best single index of a community's general health is reputed to be its infant mortality rate. For Harlem this rate in 1961 was 45.2 per 1,000 live births compared to 25.7 for New York City. For Cleveland's Hough area the infant deaths are also about double that of the rest of the city. Poor housing conditions, malnutrition, and inadequate health care are undoubtedly responsible; where flies and maggots breed, where the plumbing is stopped up and not repaired, where rats bite helpless infants, the conditions of life are brutal and inhuman. All are symptoms of the underlying fact of poverty. Perhaps even more extraordinary than the high rate of disease and death is the fact that so many human beings do survive.

The effect of housing upon the social and psychological well-being of its occupants is much discussed but less well documented. The most careful of the few relevant studies (those by Wilner, Walkley, Pinkerton and Tayback) on the psychological effects of poor housing have produced findings less dramatic than one would expect. The link between housing and mental health is not clearly established, but residents of public housing do have higher morale and greater pride in their neighborhoods than those who live in slums, and they are more likely to say that they have improved their lot in life and are "rising in the world." Nevertheless, their pride is generally not followed by genuine aspiration. They often express hope, but it usually is, alas, a pseudohope unaccompanied by an actual struggle to win better jobs, to get their children into college, to buy homes. Real hope is based on expectations of success; theirs seems rather a forlorn dream. Wilner and Walkley point out that

> for all the housing improvement, many other circumstances that would be expected to affect the way of life [of these families] remained substantially the same. These were still families at the lowest end of the economic scale; practical family situations remained materially unimproved; in one-third of the families there was no husband present; and one-third were on public welfare.

Housing alone does not lead to sound psychological adjustment, for to build new housing or to spruce up the old is not to abolish the multiple pathology of the slums. Still, at the very least, good housing improves health, lifts morale, and thereby helps to generate a restless eagerness for change, if not in the adult generation, then in their children, a fact, incidentally, that might give pause to some of those in society who support aid to public housing believing it will decrease the demands of Negroes. It will, in fact, stimulate them to further demands, spurred by hope for a further identification with middle-class society. Housing is no abstract social and political problem, but an extension of a man's personality. If the Negro has to identify with a rat-infested tenement, his sense of personal inadequacy and inferiority, already aggravated by job discrimination and other forms of humiliation, is reinforced by the physical reality around him. If his home is clean and decent and even in some way beautiful, his sense of self is stronger. A house is a concrete symbol of what the person is worth.

In Harlem, a Haryou interviewer had a conversation with a little girl about her home that revealed both the apathy and the hope of the ghetto:

> *Interviewer.* Tell me something about you—where you were born, you know, where you grew up, how everything went for you?
>
> *Gwen D.* When I was born I lived on 118th Street. There was a man killed in the hallway, and a man died right in front of the door where I lived at. My mother moved after that man got killed.
>
> I liked it in 97th Street because it was integration in that block. All kinds of people lived there.
>
> *Interviewer.* Spanish people? White people?
>
> *Gwen D.* Spanish people, Italian people, all kinds of people. I liked it

because it wasn't one group of whites and one group of Negroes or Spanish or something like that; everybody who lived in that block were friends.

Interviewer. How come you moved?

Gwen D. Well, my mother she didn't like the building too well.

Interviewer. What didn't she like about it?

Gwen D. Well, it was falling down!

Interviewer. In your whole life, has anything happened to you that you really got excited about?

Gwen D. I can't remember.

Interviewer. Tell me about some real good times you've had in your life.

Gwen D. In Harlem?

Interviewer. In your life, that you've really enjoyed.

Gwen D. One year we was in summer school, and we went to this other school way downtown, out of Harlem, to give a show, and everybody was so happy. And we were on television, and I saw myself, and I was the only one there with a clean shirt and blouse.

Interviewer. And you really got excited about that. Anything else ever happen to you that you had a really good time?

Gwen D. No.

Interviewer. What kind of changes would you want to make? Changes so that you can have a better chance, your sisters can have a better chance and your brother?

Gwen D. Well, I just want a chance to do what I can.

6 THE FAIR HOUSING ACT OF 1968

Several aspects of problems related to the civil rights movement of the 1950s and 1960s were reflected in an omnibus measure enacted by Congress in April of 1968. Among other things the measure prohibited the intimidation of civil rights workers and the crossing of state lines with the intent to incite a riot. Title VIII of the act, however, was a far-ranging effort to prevent racial discrimination in the sale or rental of housing.

From 82 Stat. 73 (1968).

Sec. 801. It is the policy of the United States to provide, within constitutional limitations, for fair housing throughout the United States. . . .

EFFECTIVE DATES OF CERTAIN PROHIBITIONS

Sec. 803. (a) Subject to the provisions of subsection (b) and section 807, the prohibitions against discrimination in the sale or rental of housing set forth in section 804 shall apply:

(1) Upon enactment of this title, to—

(A) dwellings owned or operated by the Federal Government;

(B) dwellings provided in whole or in part with the aid of loans, advances, grants, or contributions made by the Federal Government, under agreements entered into after November 20, 1962, unless payment due thereon has been made in full prior to the date of enactment of this title;

(C) dwellings provided in whole or in part by loans insured, guaranteed, or otherwise secured by the credit of the Federal Government, under agreements entered into after November 20, 1962, unless payment thereon has been made in full prior to the date of enactment of this title: *Provided,* That nothing contained in subparagraphs (B) and (C) of this subsection shall be applicable to dwellings solely by virtue of the fact that they are subject to mortgages held by an FDIC or FSLIC institution; and

(D) dwellings provided by the development or the redevelopment of real property purchased, rented, or otherwise obtained from a State or local public agency receiving Federal financial assistance for slum clearance or urban renewal with respect to such real property under loan or grant contracts entered into after November 20, 1962.

(2) After December 31, 1968, to all dwellings covered by paragraph (1) and to all other dwellings except as exempted by subsection (b).

(b) Nothing in section 804 (other than subsection (c)) shall apply to—

(1) any single-family house sold or rented by an owner: *Provided,* That such private individual owner does not own more than three such single-family houses at any one time: *Provided further,* That in the case of the sale of any such single-family house by a private individual owner not residing in such house at the time of such sale or who was not the most recent resident of such house prior to such sale, the exemption granted by this subsection shall apply only with respect to one such sale within any twenty-four month period: *Provided further,* That such bona fide private individual owner does not own any interest in, nor is there owned or reserved on his behalf, under any express or voluntary agreement, title to or any right to all or a portion of the proceeds from the sale or rental of, more than three such single-family houses at any one time: *Provided further,* That after

December 31, 1969, the sale or rental of any such single-family house shall be excepted from the application of this title only if such house is sold or rented

(A) without the use in any manner of the sales or rental facilities or the sales or rental services of any real estate broker, agent, or salesman, or of such facilities or services of any person in the business of selling or renting dwellings, or of any employee or agent of any such broker, agent, salesman, or person and

(B) without the publication, posting or mailing, after notice, of any advertisement or written notice in violation of section 804(c) of this title; but nothing in this proviso shall prohibit the use of attorneys, escrow agents, abstractors, title companies, and other such professional assistance as necessary to perfect or transfer the title, or

(2) rooms or units in dwellings containing living quarters occupied or intended to be occupied by no more than four families living independently of each other, if the owner actually maintains and occupies one of such living quarters as his residence.

(c) For the purposes of subsection (b), a person shall be deemed to be in the business of selling or renting dwellings if—

(1) he has, within the preceding twelve months, participated as principal in three or more transactions involving the sale or rental of any dwelling or any interest therein, or

(2) he has, within the preceding twelve months, participated as agent, other than in the sale of his own personal residence in providing sales or rental facilities or sales or rental services in two or more transactions involving the sale or rental of any dwelling or any interest therein, or

(3) he is the owner of any dwelling designed or intended for occupancy by, or occupied by, five or more families.

DISCRIMINATION IN THE SALE OR RENTAL OF HOUSING

Sec. 804. As made applicable by section 803 and except as exempted by sections 803(b) and 807, it shall be unlawful—

(a) To refuse to sell or rent after the making of a bona fide offer, or to refuse to negotiate for the sale or rental of, or otherwise make unavailable or deny, a dwelling to any person because of race, color, religion, or national origin.

(b) To discriminate against any person in the terms, conditions, or privileges of sale or rental of a dwelling, or in the provision of services or facilities in connection therewith, because of race, color, religion, or national origin.

(c) To make, print, or publish, or cause to be made, printed, or published any notice, statement, or advertisement, with respect to the sale or rental of a dwelling that indicates any preference, limitation, or discrimination based on race, color, religion, or national origin, or an intention to make any such preference, limitation, or discrimination.

(d) To represent to any person because of race, color, religion, or national origin that any dwelling is not available for inspection, sale, or rental when such dwelling is in fact so available.

(e) For profit, to induce or attempt to induce any person to sell or rent any dwelling by representations regarding the entry or prospective entry into the neighborhood of a person or persons of a particular race, color, religion, or national origin.

DISCRIMINATION IN THE FINANCING OF HOUSING

Sec. 805. After December 31, 1968, it shall be unlawful for any bank, building and loan association, insurance company or other corporation, association, firm or enterprise whose business consists in whole or in part in the making of commercial real estate loans, to deny a loan or other financial assistance to a person applying therefor for the purpose of purchasing, constructing, improving, repairing, or maintaining a dwelling, or to discriminate against him in the fixing of the amount, interest rate, duration, or other terms or conditions of such loan or other financial assistance, because of the race, color, religion, or national origin of such person or of any person associated with him in connection with such loan or other financial assistance or the purposes of such loan or other financial assistance, or of the present or prospective owners, lessees, tenants, or occupants of the dwelling or dwellings in relation to which such loan or other financial assistance is to be made or given: *Provided*, That nothing contained in this section shall impair the scope or effectiveness of the exception contained in section 803(b).

DISCRIMINATION IN THE PROVISION OF BROKERAGE SERVICES

Sec. 806. After December 31, 1968, it shall be unlawful to deny any person access to or membership or participation in any multiple-listing service, real estate brokers' organization or other service, organization, or facility relating to the business of selling or renting dwellings, or to discriminate against him in the terms or conditions of such access, membership, or participation, on account of race, color, religion, or national origin.

III Finding a Job

Economic opportunity—the possibility of significantly raising one's standard of living—was a major factor in inducing Negroes to move to the city. This was especially the case during the world wars, when acute shortages of labor developed in industrial areas. Initially much optimism was expressed about the prospects for employment, and compared to the rural South the wages were indeed high. But in the city the high costs sharply reduced the real gain in income. Moreover, many of the migrants lacked the skills for the better jobs, and even for those qualified the prejudices of employers and trade unions severely restricted available opportunities. While the federal government finally attempted to protect Negro workers from such discrimination, the results in the 1960s left much to be desired. Thus the continuing critically high rates of unemployment in the black ghetto contrast sharply with the optimistic expectations of earlier Negro migrants.

1   RACIAL PREJUDICE AND EMPLOYMENT OPPORTUNITY IN THE CITY OF BROTHERLY LOVE

In northern cities employment opportunities for Negroes had long been severely restricted. The situation in the Philadelphia of the 1890s is described by the distinguished Negro historian and sociologist, W. E. B. DuBois, in this selection.

From W. E. B. DuBois, The Philadelphia Negro: A Social Study *(Philadelphia: The University of Pennsylvania Press, 1899), pp. 126–29.*

The practical exclusion of the Negro from the trades and industries of a great city like Philadelphia is a situation by no means easy to explain. It is often said simply: the foreigners and trade unions have crowded Negroes out on account of race prejudice and left employers and philanthropists helpless in the matter. This is not strictly true. What the trade unions and white workmen have done is to seize an economic advantage plainly offered them. This opportunity arose from three causes: Here was a mass of black workmen of whom very few were by previous training fitted to become the mechanics and artisans of a new industrial development; here, too, were an increasing mass of foreigners and native Americans who were unusually well fitted to take part in the new industries; finally, most people were willing and many eager that Negroes should be kept as menial servants rather than develop into industrial factors. This was the situation, and here was the opportunity for the white workmen; they were by previous training better workmen on the average than Negroes; they were stronger numerically and the result was that every new industrial enterprise started in the city took white workmen. Soon the white workmen were strong enough to go a step further than this and practically prohibit Negroes from entering trades under any circumstances; this affected not only new enterprises, but also old trades like carpentering, masonry, plastering and the like. The supply of Negroes for such trades could not keep pace with the extraordinary growth of the city and a large number of white workmen entered the field. They immediately combined against Negroes primarily to raise wages; the standard of living of the Negroes lets them accept low wages, and, conversely, long necessity of accepting the meagre wages offered have made a low standard of living. Thus partially by taking advantage of race prejudice, partially by greater economic efficiency and partially by the endeavor to maintain and raise wages, white workmen have not only monopolized the new industrial opportunities of an age which has transformed Philadelphia from a colonial town to a world-city, but have also been enabled to take from the Negro workman the opportunities he already enjoyed in certain lines of work.

If now a benevolent despot had seen the development, he would immediately have sought to remedy the real weakness of the Negro's position, i.e., his lack of training; and he would have swept away any discrimination that compelled men to support as criminals those who might support themselves as workmen.

He would have made special effort to train Negro boys for industrial life and given them a chance to compete on equal terms with the best white workmen; arguing that in the long run this would be best for all concerned, since by raising the skill and standard of living of the Negroes he would make them effective workmen and competitors who would maintain a decent level of wages. He would have sternly suppressed organized or covert opposition to Negro workmen.

There was, however, no benevolent despot, no philanthropist, no far-seeing captain of industry to prevent the Negro from losing even the skill he had learned or to inspire him by opportunities to learn more. As the older Negroes with trades dropped off, there was little to induce younger men to succeed them. On the contrary special effort was made not to train Negroes for industry or to allow them to enter on such a career. Consequently they gradually slipped out of industrial life until in 1890 when the Negroes formed 4 per cent of the population, only 1.1 per cent of 134,709 men in the principal trades of the city were Negroes; of 46,200 women in these trades 1.3 per cent were Negroes; or taking men and women together, 2,160 or 1.19 per cent of all were Negroes. This does not, however, tell the whole story, for of this 2,160, the barbers, brick-makers, and dressmakers formed 1,434. In the Seventh Ward the number in the trades is much larger than the proportion in the city, but here again they are confined to a few trades—barbers, dressmakers, cigarmakers and shoemakers.

How now has this exclusion been maintained? In some cases by the actual inclusion of the word "white" among qualifications for entrance into certain trade unions. More often, however, by leaving the matter of color entirely to local bodies, who make no general rule, but invariably fail to admit a colored applicant except under pressing circumstances. This is the most workable system and is adopted by nearly all trade unions. In sections where Negro labor in certain trades is competent and considerable, the trade union welcomes them, as in Western Pennsylvania among miners and iron-workers, and in Philadelphia among cigarmakers; but whenever there is a trade where good Negro workmen are comparatively scarce each union steadfastly refuses to admit Negroes, and relies on color prejudice to keep up the barrier. Thus the carpenters, masons, painters, iron-workers, etc., have succeeded in keeping out nearly all Negro workmen by simply declining to work with non-union men and refusing to let colored men join the union. Sometimes, in time of strikes, the unions are compelled in self-defence not only to allow Negroes to join but to solicit them; this happened, for instance, in the stone-cutters' strike some years ago.

To repeat, then, the real motives back of this exclusion are plain: a large part is simple race prejudice, always strong in working classes and intensified by the peculiar history of the Negro in this country. Another part, however, and possibly a more potent part, is the natural spirit of monopoly and the desire to keep up wages. So long as a cry against "Irish" or "foreigners" was able to marshal race prejudice in the service of those who desired to keep those people out of some employments, that cry was sedulously used. So to-day the workmen plainly see that a large amount of competition can be shut off by taking advantage of public opinion and drawing the color line. Moreover, in this there is one thoroughly justifiable consideration that plays a great part: namely, the Negroes are used to low wages—can live on them, and consequently would fight less fiercely than most whites against reduction.

2   OPPORTUNITIES FOR NEGRO MIGRANTS

The demand for labor in northern industrial centers was an important factor in stimulating the great exodus from the South that began during World War I. While the migrants still encountered plenty of racial prejudice, there were employment opportunities that were quite unavailable in the South. An optimistic assessment of this condition was written in 1920 by Walter F. White, then an assistant secretary of the National Association for the Advancement of Colored People.

From Walter F. White, "The Success of Negro Migration," Crisis 19 (January, 1920): 112-15. Reprinted by permission of The Crisis Publishing Company, Inc.

So much has been said and with so little foundation in fact about the Negro migrant that an inquiry has been made by the National Association for the Advancement of Colored People into his progress in certain industrial centers of the North. These include Chicago, Pittsburgh, Detroit, Cleveland, the Atlantic Coast shipbuilding plants, the steel and manufacturing sections of Pennsylvania, Ohio, and adjoining states.

In Chicago 40,000 colored men and 12,000 women have been added to the industrial population since the migration began. According to T. Arnold Hill of the Chicago Urban League, the stockyards employ 8,000 of these; the Corn Products Refining Company has increased its force of colored employees in one year from 30 to 800; the International Harvester Company employs 500; and the Pullman Car Shops, 400. The Industrial Department of the Urban League places about 1,000 a month. Many of the industrial plants endeavor to maintain a ratio of one Negro to every three white workmen, although the population ratio in Chicago is one Negro to thirty whites. The outlook for retention of this labor is excellent, according to all reports, and no encouragement was given to southern labor agents in their efforts to induce Negroes to return. Negroes are rapidly adjusting themselves to the new industrial and social environment; they are saving money, which is evidenced by the large number of depositors in the banks located in the Second and Third Wards, where most of the colored population live; they are conducting an increasing number of business enterprises, and real estate dealers are reaping a rich harvest in selling homes to Negroes. In spite of the serious rioting of July and August, there is yet a marked influx into the city and jobs are secured with little difficulty for all who want to work. Employers who have had no experience before with Negro labor are, in the main, finding that the old belief about the inefficiency of Negro labor is a myth. The greatest proof of this is the eagerness with which colored applicants for jobs are received.

In Pittsburgh competent observers, who are in close touch with labor conditions, state that fully 12,000 Negroes have been placed during the past two and a half years. One large employer of labor states that Negro labor as a whole is far superior to any type of immigrant labor which he has used. Thrown into the rigorous industrial life, working in mills with roaring machinery overhead and all around him, the man who has been used only to the quiet life of the rural South finds it difficult at first to adjust himself to the new order of things. Yet the testimony is almost unanimous that after a period of adjustment, the vast majority soon shake off habits of tardiness, of indolence, of unreliability, and of carousing at night, and are rapidly absorbed into the industrial life. It is evident in Pittsburgh that prohibition has had a beneficial effect, for there is less disorder and savings bank deposits are growing larger. All signs indicate a bright outlook for the retention of those who have already come and many more who are planning to come North.

Five thousand migrants have been placed in Cleveland. Recently a questionnaire was sent to 150 industrial plants, asking for specific information on the question of the efficiency of migrant labor. Practically all of the questionnaires were answered and only a few expressed any dissatisfaction. In the main, the answers were highly laudatory, and due to rigid citizenship requirements which employers have adopted, the outlook is exceptionally good for the Negro in preference to the immigrant population upon which employers have been largely dependent in the past.

One Detroit automobile firm employs some 1,200 to 1,500 Negroes. Another similar plant employs over 1,100. In this latter plant a most interesting situation has taken place, which is a valuable commentary on the efficiency and adaptability of Negro labor. In one of the departments of this establishment prior to the introduction of Negro labor, 70 white men of various nationalities were producing an average of 18 chassis a day. The official records of this plant show that within six weeks after an all-Negro force was placed in this department, 50 men were turning out from 40 to 50 a day—a clear gain in efficiency of over 300 per cent. Another blow to the exponents of the doctrine of race inferiority!

According to Dr. George E. Haynes, of the Department of Labor, 24,647 Negroes were employed in shipbuilding on the Atlantic Coast during the war and 14,075 since the war ended. Of this number a large percentage was employed in those lines of employment classed as skilled labor, and this number is increasing as the Negro is given the opportunity to prove his worth.

All of the above testimony is but a fragment of the record being made by the migrant. As long as the tide of immigration is turned away from America rather than toward it, he will be able to enter into northern industry in ever increasing numbers. Further factors are the efficiency of his labor, the attitude of labor unions and non-labor union groups, and his absorption into the industrial, economic, and social life of the North. The one question which confronts Negro labor is that of his making good and continuing to do so. Without attempting to moralize, if he does make good and if the migration continues to bring more colored labor into the North, the difficulties which he now confronts in overcoming a mythical and slanderous propaganda of untruths as to his worth will be gradually, but surely, overcome. There is great opportunity in the North for men and women who are willing to work and the southern employers of labor may as well abandon all hopes they may be cherishing of inducing the Negro to return. The American Federation of Labor has, on paper at least, abolished the color line. This forms an excellent barometer as to the future of Negro labor, but that barring of the color line in the A. F. of L., or any other organization of labor, will only be permanent when Negroes make good in large numbers and present their case in strong enough terms to force consideration and recognition.

According to all visible signs, the Negro migrant has made good, the migration is still going on, and will continue to go on until the industrial needs of the North are supplied and the South can learn to accord to the Negro all the privileges he demands. Some raving demagogues of that section may declare that this will never be. Their statements do not interest the Negro, however, and the time may yet come when the South will awaken from its dream of hordes of disillusioned Negroes flocking back to their "best friends," and will realize the gold mine of Negro labor which it had and lost.

3 UNEMPLOYMENT DURING THE GREAT DEPRESSION

The restrictions on Negro job opportunities were damaging enough during good times. With the economic collapse of the 1930s, however, black workers suffered more than any other group. This selection describes some of the difficulties encountered in the cities in 1931, a year or more before the peak of unemployment had been reached.

From National Urban League, Unemployment Status of Negroes: A Compilation of Facts and Figures Respecting Unemployment Among Negroes in One Hundred and Six Cities (*New York: National Urban League, December 1931*), pp. 11, 12, 23, 24, 32, 39, 40. Reprinted by permission of the National Urban League.

BIRMINGHAM

Unemployment among Negroes is believed to be worse than during any previous industrial shrinkage. Lodges, churches, and schools have been "greatly upset because of the financial shortage brought on by unemployment of large numbers."

Some of the largest and best equipped churches are at present without pastors because the members, both men and women, are without work and therefore without money to support their pastors. Industrial and straight-life policies have lapsed in large numbers. Wages have been cut for both whites and Negroes. Robbery and theft are common. "Many poor children of unemployed parents can be seen daily on the city dump hunting for cast-away foods or bread that has been sent out by grocers as not being fit for food."

LOS ANGELES

Unemployment is on the increase. At one office, out of 180 registrants for October only 15 were placed in jobs. November showed a steady increase in registrants with few or no orders for workers.

The Negro transient boy is a problem. He is part of the general influx to the city because of California's mild climate. It is expected that funds will be made available to take care of the boy problem.

The county has been fair in allocating jobs to Negro unemployed when it has direct charge of its work. Contractors who work on county jobs give few places to Negroes. Subtle excuses are being manufactured in order to justify the discharge of Negroes and the placement of whites in their stead. A case in point is a large cleaning establishment in the Negro district which though it has hired members of this race for a period of 18 or 20 years has dismissed them. The reason given in this case is a familiar one, namely that whites were substituted for Negroes when there was a change in management. Such practices have made for a general attitude of hopelessness and despair on the part of a large number of those applying for work. Some are attentive to radical propaganda, but the number is at present small.

BOSTON

There are between 3,000 and 5,000 Negroes out of work in Greater Boston. The Boston Negro in the unemployed class offers a serious problem to the welfare authorities who have noticed a marked reluctance on the part of the black man to ask for charity relief. While demands for jobs increase daily it is still a curious fact that requests for relief are not in proportion to those known to be out of work and in serious straits. Two reasons are advanced for this situation—one is that the Negro here has provided some means for helping himself through such crises as these, or he has determined to suffer while searching for work.

One situation which has helped the Negro laborer to some extent is the Longshoreman's strike which has thrown about 600 jobs to Negroes which ordinarily would go to white Union men. This is causing strained relations between black and white workmen in this field, but it also is offering jobs to many who would be without them.

DETROIT

The Negro in this highly industrialized city forms 7 per cent of the population, and in normal times is 20 per cent of the dependency group. Today, with unemployment holding sway, and more than 200,000 people out of work the Negro is 30 per cent of the dependency group. An official of the City of Detroit feels that the Negro is the last person hired in factories and in other forms of industry, and is usually the first to be fired when business begins to shake as it has done throughout the past twenty-four months. Negroes are participating in Communistic movements, Detroit officials admit, but they do not show any unusual radical tendencies.

The problem among Negroes has been so great that the agency charged with the responsibility of taking care of their industrial problems has been "up to its neck" in trying to provide further participation. Recently from 700 to 800 Negroes, former employees of one of the automobile companies, were recalled for employment.

MANHATTAN

It is estimated that there are between 35,000 and 40,000 colored workers unemployed in Harlem. (While this is the largest congregation of Negroes many others live in other parts of the city.) At this writing, November 27, only 4,612 men have registered at the 135th Street office of the Emergency Committee and 2,906 women at the 137th Street registration office. No figures indicating how many of these workers have been placed are available. It is known, however, that some are going to work but it is the general feeling that too many ineligible for support from relief agencies are unable to find employment. The unskilled worker, whether of high school, college or ungraded development, is suffering greatly. Public agencies are using women as clerks, nurses have gone to work for hospitals, and men are working on noncompetitive operations— all of these being paid by the Emergency Relief Fund.

Undoubtedly domestic and personal service workers are losing jobs they once held. These places are now filled by white workers. Some compensation for this, however, is provided by companies that are using salesmen in stores and for door-to-door canvassing, the civil service and other forms of employment.

New York, of course, is regarded as a hot-bed for radicalism. Not a few Negroes take part in meetings on street corners, in buildings, park demonstrations and parades. Their interest pivots around the failure of Negroes to find work commensurate with their ability and it is around the resentment of Negroes on this point that Communistic agitators have built their case.

Agencies in New York were slow in appointing Negro case workers for emergency relief projects. The Welfare Council and the Emergency Work Bureau were severely criticised because of their decision to establish two offices in Harlem under the general supervision of a white professional worker. The placing of interviewers and case workers under white supervisors has partially met criticisms which relief officials felt unjustified because of their failure to find capable Negro social workers to man the offices. That there were no trained workers of this type is partly explained by the fact that the regular relief agencies have not employed Negro case workers. In fact at the time the contention was made the two chief agencies had not over two in their employ.

PHILADELPHIA

Estimates place Philadelphia's unemployed close to 247,000 persons, of whom between 30,000 and 50,000 are Negroes.

The Bureau of Unemployment Relief, the agency that handles over 90 per cent of the relief work throughout the city, had a case load during November of 34,036 families, of which 15,387 were colored. The percentage of colored families for the two months previous remained between 44 per cent and 46 per cent of the total, although Negroes form but 11.3 per cent of the total population of the city. No differences are made on account of race. The size and financial circumstances of the family determines the extent of relief. Of a total of 182 workers employed by the Bureau, 25 are Negroes.

The Shelter for Homeless Men reopened again this year. On November 15 of a total registration of 1,417, there were 663 Negroes, or 28.7 per cent. A more rigid policy has been adopted this year in ascertaining and treating transients. Our correspondent writes:

> "The method used this year by the Bureau of Emergency Relief by which aid is administered directly to needy families in the form of grocery orders has done much to preserve and restore homes and thereby has reduced the number of Homeless Men. Agencies heretofore had been more partial to deserted families, and in a number of cases husbands pulled off from their families, taking refuge at the Shelter, feeling that the ones left behind would create more sympathy and fare much better without them." Decreases in contributions, membership fees, and gifts to philanthropic organizations are noted, as is decrease in financial aid to churches.

Numerous instances are noticed of discharges and replacements of Negro workers, the customary excuses being given such as "inefficiency," "impudence," and "white customers object to the counter service of some darker skinned maids."

Only a passive interest is being shown by Negroes in radical movements.

4 ROOSEVELT ESTABLISHES THE F.E.P.C.

During the 1930s the federal government asserted a policy of equal employment opportunity either by executive action or by provisions in many of the New Deal laws. Unfortunately, this had only limited effect in practice. By the early 1940s Negroes became increasingly vocal in demanding an end to job discrimination in the expanding defense industries. Threatened by a massive Negro march on Washington, led by A. Philip Randolph, president of the Brotherhood of Sleeping Car Porters, President Roosevelt issued Executive Order No. 8802 on June 25, 1941, establishing a Fair Employment Practices Committee. The committee was weak, however, and was reconstituted and strengthened by a second order in 1943. The original order is reprinted here.

From 6 Federal Register *3109.*

WHEREAS it is the policy of the United States to encourage full participation in the national defense program by all citizens of the United States, regardless of race, creed, color, or national origin, in the firm belief that the democratic way of life within the Nation can be defended successfully only with the help and support of all groups within its borders; and

WHEREAS there is evidence that available and needed workers have been barred from employment in industries engaged in defense production solely because of considerations of race, creed, color, or national origin, to the detriment of workers' morale and of national unity:

NOW, THEREFORE, by virtue of the authority vested in me by the Constitution and the statutes, and as a prerequisite to the successful conduct of our national defense production effort, I do hereby reaffirm the policy of the United States that there shall be no discrimination in the employment of workers in defense industries or government because of race, creed, color, or national origin, and I do hereby declare that it is the duty of employers and of labor organizations, in furtherance of said policy and of this order, to provide for the full and equitable participation of all workers in defense industries, without discrimination because of race, creed, color, or national origin;

And it is hereby ordered as follows:

1. All departments and agencies of the Government of the United States concerned with vocational and training programs for defense production shall take special measures appropriate to assure that such programs are administered without discrimination because of race, creed, color, or national origin;

2. All contracting agencies of the Government of the United States shall include in all defense contracts hereafter negotiated by them a provision obligating the contractor not to discriminate against any worker because of race, creed, color, or national origin;

3. There is established in the Office of Production Management a Committee on Fair Employment Practice, which shall consist of a chairman and four other members to be appointed by the President. The Chairman and members of the Committee shall serve as such without compensation but shall be entitled to actual and necessary transportation, subsistence and other expenses incidental to performance of their duties. The Committee shall receive and investigate complaints of discrimination in violation of the provisions of this order and shall take appropriate steps to redress grievances which it finds to be valid. The Committee shall also recommend to the several departments and agencies of the Government of the United States and to the President all measures which may be deemed by it necessary or proper to effectuate the provisions of this order.

FRANKLIN D. ROOSEVELT

THE WHITE HOUSE,

June 25, 1941.

5 RACISM WITHIN ORGANIZED LABOR

*The anti-Negro attitude found by DuBois in trade unions in
Philadelphia in the 1890s could still be seen among some labor unions
in the 1950s and 1960s. Examples of this problem are described by
Herbert Hill, the Labor Secretary of the NAACP.*

*From Herbert Hill, "Racism Within Organized Labor: A Report of
Five Years of the AFL-CIO, 1955–1960," The Journal of Negro
Education 30, No. 2 (Spring 1961): 109–18. Reprinted by
permission of The Bureau of Educational Research, Howard University,
and of Herbert Hill.*

The elimination of racism within trade unions was one of the major goals for organized labor announced at the merger convention of the American Federation of Labor and the Congress of Industrial Organizations in December, 1955. This was welcomed by many civil rights agencies and especially by the National Association for the Advancement of Colored People which offered its full support to the labor movement.

Today, five years after the AFL-CIO merger, the national labor organization has failed to eliminate the broad pattern of racial discrimination and segregation in many important affiliated unions. Trade union activity in the civil rights field since the merger has not been marked by a systematic and coordinated effort by the national labor federation to eliminate discrimination and segregation within local unions. This is especially true of the craft unions in the building and construction trades where the traditional anti-Negro practices basically remain in effect.

Efforts to eliminate discriminatory practices within trade unions have been piecemeal and inadequate and usually the result of protest by civil rights agencies acting on behalf of Negro workers. The National AFL-CIO has repeatedly refused to take action on its own initiative. In too many cases years have elapsed between the filing of a complaint by an aggrieved worker and acknowledgment and investigation by the Federation, if indeed there is any action at all.

Discriminatory racial practices by trade unions are not simply isolated or occasional expressions of local bias against colored workers, but rather, as the record indicates, a continuation of the institutionalized pattern of anti-Negro employment practices that is traditional with large sections of organized labor and industrial management.

The pattern of union responsibility for job discrimination against Negroes is not limited to any one area of the country or to some few industries or union jurisdictions but involves many unions in a wide variety of occupations in manufacturing industries, skilled crafts, railroads and maritime trades. . . .

AFL-CIO affiliated unions are today guilty of discriminatory racial practices in four categories: outright exclusion of Negroes, segregated locals, separate racial seniority lines in collective bargaining agreements and exclusion of Negroes from apprenticeship training programs controlled by labor unions.

As for the Federation's Civil Rights Department, its performance would seem to indicate that its major function is to create a "liberal" public relations image rather than to attack the broad pattern of anti-Negro practices within affiliated unions. The Civil Rights Committee of the AFL-CIO is the only standing committee in the Federation whose chairman is not a member of the Federation's Executive Council and/or the president of an international union. The rigid protocol of the national labor federation indicates that such a person is not in a position to impose a policy upon an international or local union but must confine himself to issuing declarations and to exercising such persuasion as he can muster. More often than not, his efforts are fruitless. . . .

SEGREGATED LOCAL UNIONS

The Brotherhood of Railway and Steamship Clerks which maintains many segregated local lodges in Northern as well as Southern cities is among the important international unions which maintain a broad national pattern of segregation. In the Brotherhood the existence of more than 150 segregated all-Negro locals with separate racial seniority rosters limits job mobility and violates the seniority rights of thousands of Negro union members.

This union has persisted in its racist practices despite repeated protests from Negro workers and community organizations. On April 30, 1957, the New York State Commission Against Discrimination ordered the merger of the "lily-white" George M. Harrison Lodge (783) and the all-Negro Friendship Lodge (6118). The white union refused to comply and the local lodges remain segregated to this day. Similar situations exist in Chicago where Negro workers are in segregated local lodge 6132 and in Tulsa, Oklahoma, where they are in local 6257. In East St. Louis and St. Louis there are 14 all-colored lodges and 14 all-white lodges which function through segregated joint councils.

The practice of segregation is so well institutionalized in this union that the designation of the Negro lodges all over the country begins with the numeral "6." It is ironic to note that the president of the Brotherhood of Railway and Steamship Clerks, George M. Harrison, is a member of the Civil Rights Committee of the AFL-CIO and a Federation Vice President. . . .

RACIAL EXCLUSION PRACTICES

Today in virtually every large urban center in the United States Negro workers are denied employment in the major industrial and residential construction projects because they are, with some few exceptions, barred from membership in the building trades craft unions. This includes the International Brotherhood of Electrical Workers, the Operating Engineers, Iron and Structural Steel Workers, Plumbers and Pipe Fitters Union, Plasterers and Lathers, the Sheet Metal Workers Union, the Boiler Makers, etc.

The basic fact of craft unions in the building trades industry is that they control access to employment by virtue of their rigid control of the hiring process. In this industry unions perform certain managerial functions, especially the assignment of union members to jobs. The refusal to admit

Negroes into membership simply denies Negro workers opportunities to secure employment.

This is true in many cities across the country such as Terre Haute, Indiana, Washington, D.C., St. Louis, Mo., Dallas, Texas, Cleveland, Ohio, East St. Louis, Ill., and Dade County, Florida, etc. (Chicago, Ill., appears to be a partial exception, perhaps because of the Negro's effective use of his growing political power.) Because the National Labor Relations Board has done little to enforce the anti-closed shop provisions of the Taft-Hartley Act, building trades unions affiliated to the AFL-CIO in most instances are closed unions operating closed shops.

Local 26 of the International Brotherhood of Electrical Workers in Washington, D.C., is a typical example of how union power is used to completely exclude Negro workers from securing employment in vast federal construction projects. For many years Negro workers have been attempting to secure admission into Local 26, which controls all hiring for electrical installation work in the Nation's capital. They have filed complaints with the President's Committee on Government Contracts which over three years ago brought this matter to the attention of the National AFL-CIO.

As of January 1, 1960, there were still no Negroes admitted into membership in Local 26. However, after the Justice Department threatened action and as a concession to pressure from other government agencies and to protests from Negro civil rights organizations, one Negro electrician, James Holland, was reluctantly permitted by the union to work in a government installation.

Soon after the merger in 1955 two international unions were admitted into the Federation with "lily-white" exclusion clauses in their constitutions although this action was clearly in violation of the policies announced at the time of the merger agreement between the AFL and the CIO. They were the International Brotherhood of Locomotive Firemen and Enginemen and the Brotherhood of Railroad Trainmen.

Since then the Brotherhood of Railroad Trainmen has removed the "Caucasian Only Clause" from its constitution but in November, 1958, the Brotherhood of Locomotive Firemen and Enginemen successfully defended its exclusion of Negroes from union membership in a suit brought by Negro firemen in the Federal District Court in Cincinnati, Ohio. Despite many appeals the National AFL-CIO refused to intervene or make any public comment and this union continues to exclude all Negroes from membership.

For almost a generation qualified Negro plumbers have been attacking the racial exclusion practices of the Plumbers Union (United Association of Journeymen and Apprentices of the Plumbing and Pipe Fitting Industry of the United States and Canada, AFL-CIO). On December 4, 1958, Frank T. Lyerson submitted an affidavit to the AFL-CIO Civil

Rights Department charging that Local 630 of the Plumbers Union in East St. Louis, Illinois, refused membership to him and other qualified Negroes. Although Local 630 limits membership to white persons exclusively, the National AFL-CIO has not taken any action on this or on other complaints against the Plumbers Union.

The practices of other building trades unions in the St. Louis-East St. Louis area are typical of the racial exclusion practices of many old-line craft unions. At the present time qualified Negro workers are barred from securing employment in the large harbor improvement project in St. Louis, as well as in the vast federally-financed construction programs in East St. Louis because of the exclusionist practices of unions affiliated to the Building Trades Council of the AFL-CIO.

Local 309 of the International Brotherhood of Electrical Workers, AFL-CIO, in East St. Louis is an all-white local and has consistently refused to admit qualified Negroes, including Jethro Smith who filed an affidavit with the National AFL-CIO. Henry Densmore filed a similar affidavit against the Operative Plasterers and Cement Masons Association, Local 90, which also maintains a rigid policy of excluding Negroes from membership. . . .

SEPARATE RACIAL SENIORITY LINES IN COLLECTIVE BARGAINING AGREEMENTS

Many major unions affiliated [with] the AFL-CIO have negotiated into their collective bargaining agreements separate lines of seniority promotion. These limit Negro employment to unskilled or menial labor classifications which deny Negro workers equal seniority and other rights and prevent them from developing job skills which permit employment in more desirable classifications.

Although some few isolated actions can be reported as having eliminated separate seniority lines such as that of the United Automobile Workers of America at the General Motors Fisher Body plant in St. Louis, Missouri (UAW Local 25), the action of the Oil, Chemical and Atomic Workers Union at the Magnolia Refining Corp., Beaumont, Texas, and at the Phillips Petroleum Corporation in Kansas City, Missouri, as well as the limited action by the United Steelworkers of America in response to a lawsuit filed by Negro members at the Sheffield Steel Company in Houston, Texas, the pattern of such discrimination remains practically intact in Southern industrial operations where trade unions hold collective bargaining agreements. . . .

APPRENTICESHIP TRAINING

The continued exclusion of Negroes from apprenticeship training is particularly disturbing because of rapid technological changes in the

Nation's economy. Because of the disproportionate concentration of Negroes in the unskilled sections of the labor force there has already been a disproportionate displacement of Negroes as a result of technological change. Continued exclusion of Negro youth from major apprenticeship training programs in the North as well as in the South endangers the future economic well-being of the entire Negro community.

It is important to note that in the ten-year period from 1950–1960, in the State of New York, the increase of Negro participation in building trades apprenticeship training programs rose only from 1.5 per cent to per cent. In most of these programs the role of the labor union is decisive because the trade union usually determines who is admitted into the training programs and, therefore, who is admitted into the union.

Recent studies clearly indicate that no large-scale significant advances have been made by Negroes into those craft union apprenticeship programs which have historically excluded non-whites. The railroad craft unions as well as the railroad operating brotherhoods remain adamant in their opposition to Negro craftsmen and bar apprenticeship opportunities to Negro youth.

Almost equally exclusive are the printing trades unions with exceptions being found in some areas of the Assistant Printing Pressmen Union and the Lithographers Union. Open access to plumbing and pipe fitting apprenticeships controlled by the Plumbers Union is a rare experience for a young Negro in the North as well as in the South. Similarly Negro youth are almost completely excluded from apprenticeship programs operated by the Sheet Metal Workers Union, the Ornamental and Structural Iron Workers, the Glass Workers, the Tile Setters, the Machinists or the Bricklayers Union. . . .

Increasingly, apprenticeship and other forms of technical training become the heart of fair employment practices. The continued exclusion of Negro youth from such programs, especially those controlled by AFL-CIO craft unions in the printing industry, the building and metal trades and in other craft jurisdictions prevents thousands of young persons from realizing their human potential and dooms them and their families to a marginal economic existence. It is in this area that the disparity between the public relations pronouncements of the AFL-CIO on civil rights and the day-to-day reality for Negro workers is most sharply outlined.

Many traditional sources of Negro employment (the Nation's railroads and mass-production industries, for example), are rapidly drying up as a result of automation and other technological changes in the economy. Today the status of the Negro wage earner is characterized by drastic change and crisis. Thus, the virtual exclusion of Negroes from apprenticeship and other training programs forces them to remain as marginal employees in the economy. They are the ones who are hired last and who

can be dispensed with easily with the added advantage that their di
placement can be rationalized in terms of lower attainment in craft skill

In addition, the appreciable lack of skilled Negro craftsmen directl
affects the economic well-being of the entire Negro population as
removes potential sources of high income occupations from the grou
The devices outlined briefly in this report operate effectively to conce
trate Negro wage earners in those jobs which suffer the highest instanc
of unemployment.

The concentration of unskilled, low-paying jobs with a lack of employ
ment stability together with other income limitations such as denial
access to union hiring halls in the building trades, and separate racia
lines of seniority promotion in collective bargaining agreements all co
tribute to an explanation of why Negroes constitute a permanentl
depressed economic group in American society.

6   CIVIL RIGHTS ACT OF 1964

*Title VII of the Civil Rights Act of 1964 was the culmination of a
long effort that began in the early 1940s to provide legislative protection
for the principle of equal employment opportunity. The Act was passed
by the Senate in June only after a filibuster was ended by the adoption
of cloture, the first such instance for a civil rights measure.*

*The following summary was prepared by the U.S. Commission on
Civil Rights for its* Civil Rights Digest, *Special Bulletin, August,
1964.*

TITLE VII
EQUAL EMPLOYMENT OPPORTUNITY

This title establishes a Federal right to equal opportunity in employ
ment. It creates an Equal Employment Opportunity Commission to assis
in implementing this right.

Employers, labor unions and employment agencies are required t
treat all persons without regard to their race, color, religion, sex, o
national origin. This treatment must be given in all phases of employ
ment, including hiring, promotion, firing, apprenticeship and other train
ing programs, and job assignments.

When this title goes into full effect employers will be subject to its provisions if they have 25 or more regular employees in an industry that affects interstate commerce. Generally speaking, labor unions will be subject to the Act if they either operate a hiring hall for covered employers, or if they have 25 or more members who are employed by a covered employer. Employment agencies are also included if they regularly undertake to supply employees for a covered employer.

(Enforcement of the nondiscrimination requirements for employers and unions is postponed for one year. Employers and unions with 100 or more workers will be covered beginning July 2, 1965 and coverage will be extended each year until July 2, 1968 when employers and unions with 25 workers will be covered.)

Not covered by this title are (1) public employers, (2) bona fide private clubs, (3) educational institutions with regard to employees working in educational activities and all employment in religious educational institutions, (4) employers on or near an Indian reservation with regard to preferential treatment of Indians, and (5) religious corporations, institutions, etc., with regard to employees working in connection with religious activities.

When someone believes he has been discriminated against because of race, color, religion, sex, or national origin in any phase of job placement or employment, he may bring his complaint within 90 days to the Equal Employment Opportunity Commission or to the Attorney General.

The Commission will handle his complaint directly, unless the State or locality where the alleged discrimination occurred has fair employment laws. If so, the person complaining must allow the State or local officials no more than 120 days to resolve the matter. If there is no satisfactory conclusion within this time or if the State or locality rejects the complaint before the time is up, the complainant may then go to the Commission, which is authorized to settle valid complaints by conciliation and persuasion. Nothing said during the conciliation proceedings may be made public or used as evidence without the consent of the parties.

If the Commission fails to secure compliance within a period of no more than 60 days, the individual may take his case to a Federal court. This court may appoint an attorney and may exempt the complainant from payment of certain costs. The court, in its discretion, may allow the Attorney General to enter the case.

A worker who thinks he has been discriminated against may take his complaint directly to the Attorney General, who may bring the case before a three-judge court if he believes there is a pattern or practice of resistance to this title.

If the court in either action finds discrimination, it will order the employer, employment agency or union to take corrective action, which may include hiring or reinstating employees with or without back pay.

7   UNEMPLOYMENT CONTINUES

*Despite the federal legislation to protect job opportunities, unemployment
and subemployment, as well as the low status of many jobs held by
Negroes, continued to be a critical matter in the black ghetto. The
problem is summarized in this excerpt.*

From the Report of the National Advisory Commission on Civil
Disorder *(Washington, D.C.: U.S. Government Printing Office,
1968), pp. 124–26.*

NEGRO UNEMPLOYMENT

Unemployment rates among Negroes have declined from a post-
Korean War high of 12.6 per cent in 1958 to 8.2 per cent in 1967. Among
married Negro men, the unemployment rate for 1967 was down to 3.2
per cent.

Notwithstanding this decline, unemployment rates for Negroes are still
double those for whites in every category, including married men, as they
have been throughout the postwar period. Moreover, since 1954, even
during the current unprecedented period of sustained economic growth,
unemployment among Negroes has been continuously above the 6 per
cent "recession" level widely regarded as a sign of serious economic
weakness when prevalent for the entire work force.

While the Negro unemployment rate remains high in relation to the
white rate, the number of additional jobs needed to lower this to the level
of white unemployment is surprisingly small. In 1967, approximately
3 million persons were unemployed during an average week, of whom
about 638,000, or 21 per cent, were nonwhites. When corrected for
undercounting, total nonwhite unemployment was approximately 712,000
or 8 per cent of the nonwhite labor force. To reduce the unemployment
rate to 3.4 per cent, the rate prevalent among whites, jobs must be found
for 57.5 per cent of these unemployed persons. This amounts to nearly
409,000 jobs, or about 27 per cent of the net number of new jobs added
to the economy in the year 1967 alone and only slightly more than one-
half of 1 per cent of all jobs in the United States in 1967.

THE LOW-STATUS AND LOW-PAYING
NATURE OF MANY NEGRO JOBS

Even more important perhaps than unemployment is the related problem of the undesirable nature of many jobs open to Negroes. Negro workers are concentrated in the lowest skilled and lowest paying occupations. These jobs often involve substandard wages, great instability and uncertainty of tenure, extremely low status in the eyes of both employer and employee, little or no chance for meaningful advancement, and unpleasant or exhausting duties. Negro men in particular are more than three times as likely as whites to be in unskilled or service jobs which pay far less than most:

Type of occupation	Percentage of male workers in each type of occupation, 1966		Median earnings of all male civilians in each occupation, 1965
	White	Nonwhite	
Professional, technical, and managerial	27	9	$7,603[1]
Clerical and sales	14	9	5,532[1]
Craftsmen and foremen	20	12	6,270
Operatives	20	27	5,046
Service workers	6	16	3,436
Nonfarm laborers	6	20	2,410
Farmers and farm workers	7	8	1,669[1]

[1] Average of two categories from normal Census Bureau categories as combined in data presented in *The Social and Economic Conditions of Negroes in the United States* (BLS No. 332).

This concentration in the least desirable jobs can be viewed another way by calculating the changes which would occur if Negro men were employed in various occupations in the same proportions as the male labor force as a whole (not solely the white labor force).

Thus, upgrading the employment of Negro men to make their occupational distribution identical with that of the labor force as a whole would have an immense impact upon the nature of their occupations. About 1.3 million nonwhite men—or 28 per cent of those employed in 1966—would move up the employment ladder into one of the higher status and higher paying categories. The effect of such a shift upon the incomes of Negro men would be very great. Using the 1966 job distribution, the shift

Type of occupation	Number of male nonwhite workers, 1966			
	As actually distributed[1]	If distributed the same as all male workers	Difference	
			Number	Per cent
Professional, technical, and managerial	415,000	1,173,000	+758,000	+183
Clerical and sales	415,000	628,000	+213,000	+51
Craftsmen and foremen	553,000	894,000	+341,000	+62
Operatives	1,244,000	964,000	−280,000	−23
Service workers	737,000	326,000	−411,000	−56
Nonfarm laborers	922,000	340,000	−582,000	−63
Farmers and farm workers	369,000	330,000	−39,000	−11

[1] Estimates based upon percentages set forth in BLS No. 332, p. 41.

indicated above would produce about $4.8 billion more earned income for nonwhite men alone if they received the 1965 median income in each occupation. This would be a rise of approximately 30 per cent in the earnings actually received by all nonwhite men in 1965 (not counting any sources of income other than wages and salaries).

Of course, the kind of "instant upgrading" visualized in these calculations does not represent a practical alternative for national policy. The economy cannot drastically reduce the total number of low-status jobs it now contains, or shift large numbers of people upward in occupation in any short period. Therefore, major upgrading in the employment status of Negro men must come through a faster relative expansion of higher level jobs than lower level jobs (which has been occurring for several decades), an improvement in the skills of nonwhite workers so they can obtain a high proportion of those added better jobs, and a drastic reduction of discriminatory hiring and promotion practices in all enterprises, both private and public.

Nevertheless, this hypothetical example clearly shows that the concentration of male Negro employment at the lowest end of the occupational scale is greatly depressing the incomes of U.S. Negroes in general. In fact, this is the single most important source of poverty among Negroes. It is even more important than unemployment, as can be shown by a second hypothetical calculation. In 1966, there were about 724,000 unemployed nonwhites in the United States on the average, including adults and teenagers, and allowing for the Census Bureau undercount of Negroes. If every one of these persons had been employed and had received the median amount earned by nonwhite males in 1966 ($3,864), this would have added a total of $2.8 billion to nonwhite income as a whole. If only enough of these persons had been employed at that wage to reduce nonwhite unemployment from 7.3 per cent to 3.3 per cent—the rate among whites in 1966—then the income gain for nonwhites would have totaled about $1.5 billion. But if nonwhite unemployment remained at 7.3 per cent, and nonwhite men were upgraded so that they had the same occupational distribution and incomes as all men in the labor force considered together, this would have produced about $4.8 billion in additional income, as noted above (using 1965 earnings for calculation). Thus the potential income gains from upgrading the male nonwhite labor force are much larger than those from reducing nonwhite unemployment.

This conclusion underlines the difficulty of improving the economic status of Negro men. It is far easier to create new jobs than either to create new jobs with relatively high status and earning power, or to upgrade existing employed or partly employed workers into such better quality employment. Yet only such upgrading will eliminate the fundamental basis of poverty and deprivation among Negro families.

Access to good-quality jobs clearly affects the willingness of Negro men actively to seek work. In riot cities surveyed by the Commission with the largest percentage of Negroes in skilled and semiskilled jobs, Negro men participated in the labor force to the same extent as, or greater than, white men. Conversely, where most Negro men were heavily concentrated in menial jobs, they participated less in the labor force than white men.

Even given similar employment, Negro workers with the same education as white workers are paid less. This disparity doubtless results to some extent from inferior training in segregated schools, and also from the fact that large numbers of Negroes are only now entering certain occupations for the first time. However, the differentials are so large and so universal at all educational levels that they clearly reflect the patterns of discrimination which characterize hiring and promotion practices in many segments of the economy. For example, in 1966, among persons who had completed high school, the median income of Negroes was only 73 per cent that of whites. Even among persons with an eighth-grade education, Negro median income was only 80 per cent of white median income.

At the same time, a higher proportion of Negro women than white women participates in the labor force at nearly all ages except 16 to 19. For instance, in 1966, 55 per cent of nonwhite women from 25 to 34 years of age were employed, compared to only 38 per cent of white women in the same age group. The fact that almost half of all adult Negro women work reflects the fact that so many Negro males have unsteady and low-paying jobs. Yet even though Negro women are often better able to find work than Negro men, the unemployment rate among adult nonwhite women (20 years old and over) in 1967 was 7.1 per cent, compared to the 4.3 per cent rate among adult nonwhite men.

Unemployment rates are, of course, much higher among teenagers, both Negro and white, than among adults; in fact about one-third of all unemployed Negroes in 1967 were between 16 and 19 years old. During the first 9 months of 1967, the unemployment rate among nonwhite teenagers was 26.5 per cent; for whites, it was 10.6 per cent. About 219,300 nonwhite teenagers were unemployed. About 58,300 were still in school but were actively looking for jobs.

SUBEMPLOYMENT IN DISADVANTAGED NEGRO NEIGHBORHOODS

In disadvantaged areas, employment conditions for Negroes are in a chronic state of crisis. Surveys in low-income neighborhoods of nine large cities made by the Department of Labor late in 1966 revealed that the rate of unemployment there was 9.3 per cent, compared to 7.3 per cent for Negroes generally and 3.3 per cent for whites. Moreover, a high proportion of the persons living in these areas were "underemployed," that is, they were either part-time workers looking for full-time employment, or full-time workers earning less than $3,000 per year, or had dropped out of the labor force. The Department of Labor estimated that this underemployment is $2\frac{1}{2}$ times greater than the number of unemployed in these areas. Therefore, the "subemployment rate," including both the unemployed and the underemployed, was about 32.7 per cent in the nine areas surveyed, or 8.8 times greater than the overall unemployment rate for all U.S. workers.

IV Schools

An important attraction of the city for some of the Negro migrants was the prospect of finding decent schools for their children. This hope has been only partially fulfilled. While the urban schools did have facilities that were not available in much of the rural South, they were often ill-equipped to meet the challenges presented by the rapid increase in Negro population. As the central city became more and more black, the neglect of the schools by remote public officials resulted in the deterioration of plant, equipment, and standards until the educational system in some cities was reduced to a condition of endemic crisis. Moreover, it also became apparent that many white officials in the North were quite as determined as their counterparts in the South to run essentially segregated schools, even though they were not sanctioned by law. As this section illustrates, the frustrations of black parents in the 1960s, who are desperately trying to improve the schools for their children by gaining local control, contrasts sadly with the hopes that were expressed several decades earlier.

1   EDUCATIONAL OPPORTUNITIES
IN THE NORTH IN 1921

Writing in 1921, Kelly Miller, Dean of the Junior College of Howard University, recognized the special needs of the Negro children in the northern schools, but he was optimistic about the possibilities that seemed to exist.

From Kelly Miller, "Education of the Negro in the North," Educational Review *62, No. 3 (October, 1921): 233–38.*

There are six cities in the United States with more than 100,000 negroes, all of which, with the single exception of New Orleans, are to be found north of the Potomac River. The border cities, Washington, Baltimore, St. Louis, and Kansas City have separate colored schools, following the policy of the southern states. In the other cities on the list there is no legal scholastic separation of the races. The city is the center of the educational life of the nation. The great systems of education, as well as the great seats of learning, are to be found mainly in the centers of population. A million and a half negroes, constituting 15 per cent of the race, are thus brought into intimate contact with the best educational facilities to be found anywhere in the world. In the South the negroes are found mainly in the rural districts, where school facilities are meager and inadequate, and even in the large cities of this section the provisions for colored schools fall woefully short of the up-to-date standards of a well-ordered system. In speaking of the education of the negro, we should always keep in mind the widely contrasted educational advantages of these two groups.

Negroes in the North generally are admitted to all educational facilities provided for the general community, whether supported by public funds or based upon private foundation. The people of the North have devoted much of their resources and philanthropic energy to the education of the negro in the South, while giving little or no consideration to the contingent of the race within their midst. The individual has been given an equal chance in the general educational provisions and has been expected to rise or fall according to the measure of his own merit. The rapidly increas-

ng numbers focusing in the large centers of population will inevitably
all attention to the special needs of this growing group separated in many
vays from the life of the community of which they form a part. . . .

In all of the northern cities the negro is concentrated in segregated
reas and districts. This residential segregation creates a demand for
eadership and self-direction. Large as his numbers seem, taken by them-
elves, the negro constitutes only a small percentage of the total population
xcept in several of the border cities. If they were evenly distributed
hroughout the white population, they would be practically unnoticed as
 factor in the general equation. One hundred and fifty thousand negroes
n New York in the midst of six million whites, if evenly diffused, would
ount but one in forty, and would be a negligible entity in the general life
f the metropolis. But a hundred thousand negroes in Harlem constitute
 city within a city. The racial needs of this large mass must be supplied
y their own leadership, almost as if they constituted a separate com-
nunity. Negro ministers, physicians, lawyers, editors, teachers, and busi-
ess men must conform with reasonable approximation to the prevailing
tandards of the community. This opportunity gives incentive and ambi-
ion to the youth of the race to equip themselves with the fullest educa-
ional qualifications.

In most of the northern states primary education is compulsory, so
hat every negro child, in compliance with the law, must attend the public
chools for a given period of years. In the near future we may expect that
he negro will approximate his full quota in high schools, normal schools,
echnical schools, and colleges in the great centers of population where he
s rapidly congregating.

There were more than four hundred negro graduates from high schools
n the class of 1920, and more than one hundred graduates from colleges
nd professional schools in the northern states. This indicates the rapid
rowth in enrollment of the negro in secondary as well as in higher institu-
ions. There were probably 500 negroes enrolled in colleges and profes-
ional schools of the North during the past year. This educational awak-
ning in the North indicates what may be expected in the near future.

The question naturally arises as to how far separate educational facil-
ties will be deemed advisable for the negroes in the northern cities as
heir numbers tend to increase. This is already a moot question in such
ities as Philadelphia, Pittsburgh, Cincinnati, and Chicago. In Washing-
on, Baltimore, St. Louis, and Kansas City, where separate colored schools
re maintained, there is a much larger enrollment of colored pupils in
he higher levels of instruction than in Philadelphia, New York, and Bos-
on, where the schools are mixed. The separate systems seem to invoke a
eener incentive and zest.

Will separate schools bring out the higher aspirations of the negro an lead to the unfolding of his powers and possibilities? is the question cour tered by the query. Will not scholastic separation on racial lines vitia the spirit of democracy and lower the standards of the less favored rac This controversy will doubtless engender great heat of feeling and animo ity on [the] part of both races. The final outcome should be determine in the light of the best good to the negro as well as that of the communit The purpose of the schools is to produce good and useful citizens. Th objective should transcend all theoretical question of manner or metho(And yet the great democratic ideal must be kept constantly in mind.

While the mass of the race remains in the South, the educational cent of gravity will be shifting toward the North. Ambitious youth will floc to the centers of the best educational advantage, regardless of national (racial border lines. Northern institutions are filled with white souther youth, because they find there at present better educational facilities tha the South provides. They saturate themselves with the aims and idea and acquire technical facilities of these great centers of learning, and carı the acquisition back for the assimilation of their own section. Negro yout will be actuated by the same impulse and purpose. . . .

There is also a reserved feeling that it might be well to encourage sep rate negro institutions, in order to keep too large a number of negro from entering white universities. This feeling will doubtless inure great to the benefit of negro schools in the South. It must be determined wheth the northern universities are apt to impart to negro students the soci impulse and racial aspiration requisite to the best service of the race. The institutions are not adapted to the negro's peculiar circumstances ar conditions. They are founded and fostered to meet the needs, aspiration and ambitions of the most favored white youth. The negro must grasp tł general aims and ideals and interpret and apply them to the situation ar circumstances of his own race.

The schools of the South will be patterned after those in the Nort The less-developed always pay homage to the better-perfected standard The negro will gain acquaintance with the aims, ideals, and methods (the North, and will, perforce, exploit the attainment among his own peop in the South.

In the educational world the law of supply and demand is inexorabl The demand for negroes in the higher levels of intellectual, moral, ar social leadership in the North will be relatively small as compared wi the larger field of the South. The incidental hardships and inequaliti of the southern régime will be undergone in quest of a larger field f acquired attainment, quickened by sacrificial impulse of racial reclam tion. Thus the northern movement of the negro, actuated by purely indu trial and economic motives, will yield significant educational fruitag

2 PROBLEMS AND ADVANTAGES OF PUBLIC SCHOOLS IN NORTHERN CITIES: A TENTATIVE SUMMARY

In addition to the deliberate attempts by some city officials to introduce or maintain racially segregated public schools, Negroes faced numerous other obstacles to obtaining a decent education in the North. Nevertheless, the opportunities in the northern cities were still superior to those in either the rural or the urban South, a fact pointed out by the distinguished Negro sociologist, E. Franklin Frazier, in the following selection. Writing in the 1940s, Frazier showed a scholarly objectivity but no fatal pessimism in this able summary of some of the educational advantages as well as problems of Negroes in the cities of the North.

From E. Franklin Frazier, The Negro in the United States, *rev. ed. New York: The Macmillan Company, 1957), pp. 440–46. Reprinted by permission of Crowell Collier and Macmillan, Inc. Footnotes have been omitted.*

The mass migrations of Negroes from the rural South naturally created educational as well as social problems. There was the problem of acquainting the Negro children with the physical school plants in the northern city. Then there was the problem of inducting them into the routine which has become a part of the organization and functioning of urban schools. However, the most important problem was that of adjusting the Negro children to the curriculum of the school in the northern city. First, there was much retardation. The Negro child who had been in a third or fifth grade in the South was not prepared for the same grade in the North. In the South the Negro child had attended school only from three to six or seven months during the year. Moreover, the quality of education as well as the quantity of education which he had received was far inferior to that provided in the North. In the North Negro children had to become accustomed to attending school with white children and to having white teachers. The white teachers themselves were not prepared to deal with the problems which the influx of Negroes from the South, especially the rural South, presented. In fact, the problems presented by the Negro often aroused latent attitudes and confirmed stereotyped beliefs concerning Negroes.

The immediate reaction of the white community to the problems created by the presence of large numbers of Negroes from the South was that Negroes should be restricted to segregated schools. In some cities of the North, especially those near the border states, a system of segregation came into existence despite the legal right of Negroes to attend all public schools. Because of the problems facing Negro children in northern cities many articles were written to prove the advantages of segregated schools for Negroes in the northern cities. It was argued that segregated schools offered the most realistic manner in which to deal with the Negro migrants from the South, that Negro students are inspired to achieve when they have Negro teachers, that there are more graduates from segregated high schools than from mixed high schools. Negro children were supposed to enjoy all these advantages in segregated schools while receiving the same education as white children. On the opposite side appeared articles that showed that segregated schools were always inferior, that separate schools were created by selfish race-leaders, and that they caused greater misunderstanding between the races and encouraged separation in other relations of the races.

As a matter of fact, the arguments in favor of separate schools for Negroes were often based upon certain implicit assumptions concerning Negroes. Generally they implied that . . . Negro[es were] . . . not fit associate[s] of white children or that they were inferior. Moreover, there is much hypocrisy on the part of whites who argue that separate schools should be established for the benefit of Negroes. Usually Negroes who argue for separate schools "are either citizens with sons and daughters to employ, or politicians looking for extra opportunities for petty graft and patronage." Of course, sometimes race-conscious Negroes favor segregated schools as a defensive measure. In the case of both white and Negro proponents of separate schools, there is evidence of a lack of understanding of the larger cultural problems of Negroes in the urban environment.

Before considering these problems, it is necessary to know what is the actual situation of the Negro as regards public education in northern cities. First, it should be noted that 12 northern (including western) states forbid segregation; two states, Wyoming and Indiana, have permissive legislation for separate schools; and 14 states are silent on the question of segregation. Nevertheless, there are segregated schools in the North and whether there is segregation or not is not determined by the existence of the laws forbidding segregation, the absence of such laws, or permissive legislation. Although it has not been determined statistically how many schools are segregated, one estimate gives one-fourth of the schools as segregated, one-half as being mixed schools and one-fourth as being schools in which Negroes are thoroughly integrated. A tabulation of 35 cities in 16 northern and western states indicated that there were definitely no Negro teachers in the schools of 13 cities and that there were Negro teachers in the same buildings as white teachers in 16 cities. In at least six cities Negro teachers did not teach white children; but in all of the 35 cities white teachers taught Negro children. In six of the cities Negroes were principals of Negro schools, while only in New York City and Chicago were there Negro principals of schools with white students.

The problems of the Negro in the public schools in the northern city are very similar to those of immigrant children. In the northern city, as we have seen, Negroes are generally crowded into slum areas. This is owing primarily to their poverty though their cultural background is a factor not to be overlooked. The school buildings in the areas of Negro settlement are old and overcrowded. But as in the immigrant community, there are areas in the Negro community which are differentiated on the basis of occupation, income, education, and general culture. The character of the schools in these areas reflects these differences. The Negro suffers, however, certain social handicaps which are not as great in the case of the immigrant. There is an attempt to restrict the Negro to the least desirable and lowest paid jobs. The normal expansion of the Negro population is restricted because the Negro is identified by his color. These barriers to the integration of the Negro into the urban community not only restrict his gradual integration into the school system but affect the incentives and the interest of Negro school children.

There are important factors in the cultural background of the Negro that have an unfavorable influence on the relation of the Negro children to the public school in the northern city. There is a large amount of family disorganization among Negroes in northern cities which results from the impact of city life upon the simple family organization which developed in the South. This affects not only the school attendance of Negro children and their behavior in school but it affects their learning and their interest in school. The influence of the cultural background is intensified where the Negro child is segregated and does not expect the reward of an improved economic status when he has completed his education. The situation is aggravated by the tendency on the part of vocational guidance teachers to discourage Negro students from preparing themselves for jobs other than those traditionally held by Negroes.

Despite the problems and disadvantages which Negro children face in northern cities, they have been able to acquire more education than

Negro children in southern cities. This is revealed when one compares the education of Negroes 25 years old and over in the four northern cities with Negro populations of over 100,000 with Negroes of the same age group in similar cities in the South. (See Tables 1 and 2.) Nearly twice the

Table 1   *Negro and Total Population 25 Years Old and Over, by Years of School Completed, for Four Southern Cities: 1940*

YEARS OF SCHOOL COMPLETED	Atlanta		Birmingham		Memphis		New Orleans	
	NEGRO	TOTAL	NEGRO	TOTAL	NEGRO	TOTAL	NEGRO	TOTAL
No School Years Completed	6.4	3.0	8.5	4.1	6.3	3.2	8.2	4.0
Grade School: 1 to 4 years	30.8	14.1	29.9	14.2	28.2	13.9	32.0	16.2
5 to 6 years	26.2	15.6	23.9	13.8	24.8	14.4	25.0	18.4
7 to 8 years	18.2	20.7	20.7	23.8	24.3	24.2	22.1	28.3
High School: 1 to 3 years	8.2	15.5	8.5	15.2	9.0	16.2	6.7	10.5
4 years	4.4	17.2	4.7	16.4	4.0	16.5	3.3	13.0

Table 2   *Negro and Total Population 25 Years Old and Over, by Years of School Completed, for Four Northern Cities: 1940*

YEARS OF SCHOOL COMPLETED	Chicago		Detroit		New York		Philadelphia	
	NEGRO	TOTAL	NEGRO	TOTAL	NEGRO	TOTAL	NEGRO	TOTAL
No School Years Completed	3.4	4.1	3.7	3.1	3.4	7.6	5.0	5.1
Grade School: 1 to 4 years	14.7	7.5	17.2	8.9	12.8	7.2	19.6	8.1
5 to 6 years	17.5	8.6	20.0	10.6	17.0	7.8	23.3	12.2
7 to 8 years	33.3	39.7	29.1	32.5	35.6	40.9	30.1	39.9
High School: 1 to 3 years	15.1	15.2	16.5	18.8	14.7	12.7	11.9	14.3
4 years	9.4	14.7	8.4	16.6	9.6	12.4	5.0	12.1

percentage of adult Negroes in southern cities as in northern cities have received no schooling.[1] About the same relation is found in respect to

[1] Some of the Negroes 25 years old and over in the northern cities were, of course, born in the South. If Negroes born in the North could be separated from those born in the South the differences between the cities of the two sections would be even greater than the tables indicate.

Negro adults who have completed only four years of elementary education. For example, in Chicago 15 per cent of the adult Negroes have had only four years of elementary education as compared with 30 per cent for Birmingham, Alabama. Whereas the percentages for the four southern cities vary only slightly, there is considerable variation for the northern cities. In New York City about one-eighth of the adult Negroes have completed one to four years of school whereas in Philadelphia a fifth are in this class. Moreover, the proportion of Negro adults who have had only 5 or 6 years of education in Philadelphia is close to that of southern cities. But when one considers the group with seventh or eighth grade education the difference between southern and northern cities is marked. Roughly about a third of the adult Negroes in northern cities as compared with less than a fifth in Atlanta to about a fourth in Memphis have had a seventh or eighth grade education. The same outstanding differences are found in regard to secondary education. About twice the proportion of adult Negroes in the northern cities as in the southern cities have completed one to three years or four years of high school education.

The above tables also enable us to compare the education of Negroes with that of the total population of these eight cities. In the four southern cities the proportion of Negroes without schooling is twice that of the population as a whole.[2] The proportion of Negroes without schooling in the northern cities is about the same as that of the entire population with the exception of New York City, which has a large proportion of foreign-born whites who have had no schooling. Both northern and southern cities show about the same disparity between the proportion of Negroes and the total population who have received only one to four years of education. On the other hand, the disparity between the education of Negroes and the entire population in southern cities is most striking in respect to those who have attended high school. In southern cities the proportion of Negroes with one to three years of high school education is about three-fifths the proportion for the population as a whole, while in northern cities the proportion for Negroes approximates that of the population as a whole. Even more striking is the fact that the proportion of Negroes with four years of high school education in southern cities is only one-fourth that for the total population. The proportion of Negroes with four years of high school education in northern cities ranges from one-half to three-fourths of that for the entire population.

[2] The disparity between the schooling of Negroes and whites in southern cities as compared with northern cities is even greater than is indicated by these figures since Negroes constitute a larger proportion of the population of the southern cities than of northern cities and thereby lower to a greater extent the school attainments of the population as a whole of southern cities.

3   SEGREGATION ATTACKED:
THE NEW ROCHELLE CASE

*The first important application in the North of the Supreme Court's 1954
decision against segregated public schools occurred in 1961 in a case
involving New Rochelle, New York. Although segregation was not
sanctioned by state law as it had been in the South, the determination
of the school officials to achieve similar results is made clear in District
Judge Irving R. Kaufman's ruling. The defendants appealed, but the
decision was upheld later in the year by the Circuit Court of Appeals
and review was denied by the Supreme Court.*

From 191 F. Supp. 181 (1961) Footnotes have been omitted.

IRVING R. KAUFMAN, District Judge.

Plaintiffs in this class action, proceeding through their parents, are
eleven Negro infants who were formerly enrolled in the Lincoln School,
a public elementary school operated by the defendants, the Board of Education of the City of New Rochelle, and Dr. Herbert C. Clish, that city's
Superintendent of Schools. It is admitted by the defendant that approximately 94 per cent of the pupils at Lincoln are Negroes. Plaintiffs contend
that the Board has deliberately and intentionally created and maintained
Lincoln School as a racially segregated school, and thus has violated the
Fourteenth Amendment and the principles enunciated in Brown v. Board
of Education, 1954, 347 U.S. 483, 74 S.Ct. 686, 98 L.Ed. 873.

The Board operates the elementary school system in New Rochelle by
means of the neighborhood school plan. Under this plan, as it functions in
New Rochelle, the city is divided into twelve districts, each of which is
served by a centrally located school. Pupils residing within a particular
district are required to attend the school within that district, and permission to transfer to other schools is granted by the school authorities only in
exceptional circumstances. Thus, as a result of this policy, the plaintiffs
have been compelled to attend the Lincoln School. At the start of the
1960 school term, they sought to register in other elementary schools in

the city having a more heterogeneous racial composition; permission to so register was uniformly denied, and this action then followed. During the pendency of this action, plaintiffs have withdrawn from the Lincoln School, and are receiving private tutoring.

In the fall of 1959, after much public agitation against the racial imbalance in the Lincoln School, the Board proposed to replace the present Lincoln School building, admittedly antiquated, with a modern facility on the same site to serve the same neighborhood. Financing for this proposal was approved in a referendum held on May 24, 1960. The plaintiffs view this decision by the Board as the culmination of a course of conduct designed to maintain Lincoln as a racially segregated school. They thus seek an injunction restraining the defendant from proceeding with the construction of the new school. They also seek to enjoin the Board from refusing to allow them to register in schools other than Lincoln which are not racially segregated, and from requiring them to register in the Lincoln School.

The defendant Board vigorously contends that the charge of racial segregation is absurd. Its position is that no child is compelled to attend any school in the City of New Rochelle solely on the basis of race or color. It points out that two-thirds of the Negro elementary school children in New Rochelle attend public schools other than Lincoln, and that the city's two junior high schools and one senior high school are attended by all children regardless of race. It urges that the high proportion of Negroes in the Lincoln School is a result solely of residential patterns, rather than any desire on its part to maintain Lincoln as a segregated school. With respect to its decision to rebuild Lincoln School, the Board contends that it was made only after an exhaustive study undertaken in good faith, which led it to conclude that the course chosen was the only feasible alternative. Thus, the defendant maintains that no constitutional rights of the plaintiffs have been infringed in any way. . . .

In order to comprehend the Lincoln problem, as it has evolved, familiarity with the geographic and racial character of the city of New Rochelle is necessary. The city has an elongated shape, its length from north to south being almost four times its average width. The settling of population started in the southern half of the town; in relatively recent years the northern end of the city has developed. That area, however, is now in the midst of a housing boom, and in the past ten years two new elementary schools—Ward and Davis—have been built to accommodate north end students. There are virtually no Negroes in this area. The north central part of town is served by two schools, Roosevelt in the west and Barnard in the east, with only the latter having a sizable Negro enrollment. The southern end of the city is also predominantly white in population and is served by two elementary schools—Trinity and Jefferson—which have 5 per cent and 7 per cent Negro enrollment respectively. If a line were drawn east to west across the middle of New Rochelle, the area of predominantly Negro population would be found immediately south of that line, in the south central portion of the city. The Lincoln School District lies in the center of this Negro area. Bordering Lincoln are five other elementary school districts—Mayflower, Stevenson, Washington, Columbus and Webster—all of which contain a substantial Negro population. Washington school has a Negro enrollment of greater than 50 per cent, while the Negro enrollment of the other four schools varies from approximately 17 per cent to approximately 30 per cent.

Lincoln School was built in 1898; there is no evidence as to the Negro population, if any, at that time. Marylynn G. Pierce, a member of the Board of Education, testified that there has been a tradition of a Negro school in New Rochelle for approximately one hundred years, but she did not indicate how this tradition had been inherited by the Lincoln School. Events occurring subsequent to 1930 indicate that by that time the majority of the Negro population of the city was being served by the Lincoln School. In 1930, according to the uncontradicted testimony of Bertha O. White, corroborated in part by the testimony of Mrs. Pierce, and also by official school maps, a policy of gerrymandering was instituted which led to the confining of Negroes within the Lincoln School district by redrawing the district lines to coincide with Negro population movements. . . . The testimony as to the gerrymandering revealed the following:

(1) In 1930, the Webster School was built, to the northwest of Lincoln, and thus district lines in the area were redrawn. The boundary lines between Webster and Lincoln were so drawn that, in one section, they were extended to a point directly across the street from the Lincoln School. By this arrangement, an irregular corridor, which was of white population, was carved out from Lincoln and placed in the Webster district. The result was that an area containing white students, directly adjoining the Lincoln School, was districted into the Webster School, despite the fact that this area was far closer to the Lincoln School than to Webster. It was testified that the purpose of this gerrymandering was to confine Negro pupils within the Lincoln district, while allowing whites living in the same area to attend a school which was not predominantly Negro in composition.

(2) In the ensuing years, as the Negro population increased, expanding westward from the Lincoln district, the borders of Lincoln were extended in this direction so as to contain the Negroes within them.

(3) During the same period in which the boundaries between Webster and Lincoln were being adjusted, other alterations were being made between the Lincoln district and the Mayflower district to the north, although these changes were never noted in Board minutes, nor were they

reflected on official school maps for many years. By means of these boundary changes, children living in a predominantly white area known as Rochelle Park, then located in the northeast corner of the Lincoln District, were assigned to the Mayflower School.

It is highly significant that the Board has offered no evidence to refute the testimony indicating that this gerrymandering took place. Nor, did it proffer any explanation for this conduct to negate the obvious inference of a desire to segregate. In addition, Board minutes for the period subsequent to 1930 indicate that Lincoln was considered in the community as the Negro School, and that the Board intended it to be utilized after school hours as a meeting place for the Negro community. . . .

In addition to this gerrymandering, the Board instituted further policies to assure that the Lincoln School District would remain Negro, and to relieve white children of the burden of attending a predominantly Negro school. Thus, up until 1949, white children remaining in the Lincoln district were allowed to transfer to other elementary schools. For example, in the year 1949, Board minutes indicate that 106 children residing in the Lincoln district were allowed by the Board to attend other schools. . . . This policy produced the anomaly, testified to by Mrs. White, of children living in adjoining houses attending different schools solely on the basis of their race. . . . Further, it appears, for example, that white children living south of the Lincoln School were assigned to Mayflower School, approximately half a mile north of Lincoln. Thus, they apparently had to pass Lincoln each day on their way to school. . . . The inevitable result of this transfer policy, when combined with the earlier gerrymandering, was that by January of 1949, Lincoln had become a 100 per cent Negro school. . . .

The years between 1949 and 1960 have been eleven years of agitation for New Rochelle. For eleven years, responsible civic-minded organizations and groups have urged that something be done to correct the Lincoln situation; for eleven years the Board has discussed the problem, hired experts, made surveys, and constantly reiterated its belief in racial equality and the necessity for equal opportunities. But, in these eleven years, it has taken no action whatsoever to alter the racial imbalance in the Lincoln School. It has met the problem with mere words, barren of meaning, for they were never followed by deeds.

In 1954, the Supreme Court rendered its opinion in Brown v. Board of Education, supra. This decision heralded a new epoch in the quest for equality of the individual. It called for responsible public officials throughout the country to reappraise their thinking and policies, and to make every effort to afford Negroes the more meaningful equality guaranteed to them by the Constitution. The Brown decision, in short, was a lesson in democracy, directed to the public at large and more particularly to those responsible for the operation of the schools. It imposed a legal and moral obligation upon officials who had created or maintained segregated schools to undo the damage which they had fostered. And, compliance with the Supreme Court's edict was not to be less forthright in the North than in the South; no double standard was to be tolerated. . . .

I hold that the Board of Education of New Rochelle, by its conduct in the years prior to 1949, created and established the Lincoln School as a segregated, Negro school. Thus formulated, the present case falls squarely within the plain meaning of the Brown decision.

The Board contends that since Lincoln School is not in form a component of a dual system of education for whites and Negroes such as was invalidated by Brown, and since the school contains 94 per cent Negroes rather than 100 per cent Negroes, there can be no violation of the Fourteenth Amendment or of the Brown principles. But, this contention misconstrues the underlying premise of the Brown rationale. That opinion while dealing with a state-maintained dual system of education, was premised on the factual conclusion that a segregated education created and maintained by official acts had a detrimental and deleterious effect on the educational and mental development of the minority group children. The unanimous Court, speaking through Chief Justice Warren, declared that segregation of Negro children, especially in their formative years "generates a feeling of inferiority as to their status in the community that may affect their hearts and minds in a way unlikely ever to be undone." . . . The Court further emphasized the necessity of giving these minority group children the opportunity for extensive contact with other children at an early stage in their educational experience, finding such contact to be indispensable if children of all races and creeds were to become inculcated with a meaningful understanding of the essentials of our democratic way of life. That the benefits inherent in an integrated education are essential to the proper development of all children has been reiterated time and again by the many witnesses in the present case, including those called by the defendant.

With these principles clear in mind, I see no basis to draw a distinction, legal or moral, between segregation established by the formality of a dual system of education, as in Brown, and that created by gerrymandering of school district lines and transferring of white children as in the instant case. . . . The result is the same in each case: the conduct of responsible school officials has operated to deny to Negro children the opportunities for a full and meaningful educational experience guaranteed to them by the Fourteenth Amendment. Further, the fact that the Lincoln School contains approximately 6 per cent whites, surely cannot divest Lincoln of its segregated character. In a community such as New Rochelle, the presence of some 29 white children certainly does not afford the 454 Negro children in the school the educational and social contacts and interaction envisioned by Brown.

Having created a segregated school, the Constitution imposed upon the Board the duty to end segregation, in good faith, and with all deliberate speed. It is patently clear that this obligation has not been fulfilled.

The Board argues that the study which it has given to the problem, and the surveys which it has requested, conclusively indicate its good faith. But, history is made, and constitutional rights vindicated, by deeds, not by talk, resolutions, and fine phrases. As already indicated, the Board has discussed the problem, hired experts, made surveys, and constantly reiterated verbally its belief in racial equality and the necessity for equal opportunities. But the fact remains that, in eleven years, not one single act was taken to implement these expressed principles. . . .

The defendant argues, however, that the neighborhood school policy is a reasonable and educationally sound one, and thus that it is not violating the Constitution in adhering to it. But, this argument ignores the essential nature of the plaintiffs' position. They are not attacking the concept of the neighborhood school as an abstract proposition. They are, rather, attacking its application so as to deny opportunities guranteed to them by the Constitution. . . . The neighborhood school policy certainly is not sacrosanct. It is valid only insofar as it is operated within the confines established by the Constitution. It cannot be used as an instrument to confine Negroes within an area artificially delineated in the first instance by official acts. If it is so used, the Constitution has been violated and the courts must intervene. . . .

THE DECREE

In determining the manner in which the Negro children residing within the Lincoln district are to be afforded the opportunities guaranteed by the Constitution, I will follow the procedure authorized by the Supreme Court in Brown v. Board of Education, 1955, 349 U.S. 294, 75 S.Ct. 753, 99 L.Ed. 1083, and utilized by many district courts in implementing the Brown principles. Thus, I deem it unnecessary at this time to determine the extent to which each of the items of relief requested by plaintiffs will be afforded. Instead, the Board is hereby ordered to present to this Court, on or before April 14, 1961, a plan for desegregation in accordance with this Opinion, said desegregation to begin no later than the start of the 1961–62 school year. This court will retain jurisdiction of this action until such plan has been presented, approved by the court, and then implemented.

The foregoing Opinion will constitute the court's findings of fact and conclusions of law.

4   THE CRISIS IN THE GHETTO SCHOOLS

*Although official policy favors integrated schools, in practice the
tendency has been toward more, not less, racial segregation in many
northern cities. Meanwhile the need to improve the quality of the ghetto
schools becomes ever more pressing. The crisis in these schools in the
1960s is described by Kenneth B. Clark.*

From Kenneth B. Clark, Dark Ghetto: Dilemmas of Social Power
*(New York: Harper & Row, Publishers, 1965), pp. 111–18. Copyright
© 1965 by Kenneth B. Clark. Reprinted by permission of Harper &
Row, Publishers, and Victor Gollancz, Ltd. Footnotes have been omitted.*

The public schools in America's urban ghettos also reflect the oppressive
damage of racial exclusion. School segregation in the South had, for
generations, been supported by law; in the North, segregation has been
supported by community custom and indifference. It is assumed that children should go to school where they live, and if they live in segregated
neighborhoods, the schools are, as a matter of course, segregated. But the
educational crisis in the ghettos is not primarily, and certainly not exclusively, one of the inequitable racial balance in the schools. Equally serious
is the inferior quality of the education in those schools. Segregation and
inferior education reinforce each other. Some persons take the position
that the first must go before the second does; others, that the reverse is
true. What is clear is that the problem of education in the urban ghetto
seems to be a vicious cycle: If children go to school where they live and if
most neighborhoods are racially segregated, then the schools are necessarily segregated, too. If Negroes move into a previously white community
and whites then move away or send their children to private or parochial
schools, the public schools will continue to be segregated. If the quality
of education in Negro schools is inferior to that in white schools, whites
feel justified in the fear that the presence of Negroes in their own school
would lower its standards. If they move their own children away and the
school becomes predominantly Negro, and therefore receives an inferior
quality of education, the pattern begins all over again. The cycle of systematic neglect of Negro children must be broken, but the powerlessness

of the Negro communities and the fear and indifference of the white community have combined so far to keep the cycle intact.

The central questions that lie behind the entire network of problems are these: Are Negroes such—in terms of innate incapacity *or* environmental deprivation—that their children are less capable of learning than are whites, so that any school that is permitted to become integrated necessarily declines in quality? Or has inferior education been systematically imposed on Negroes in the nation's ghettos in such a way as to compel poor performance from Negro children—a performance that could be reversed with quality education? The answer[s] to these questions [are] of fundamental importance because the flight of whites from the urban public school system in many American cities is based on the belief that the first is true and the second false. If the first is false and the second true—and the centers of power in the white community can be convinced of that fact—one of the basic injustices in American life could be corrected.

THE PUBLIC SCHOOLS: A SEGREGATED SYSTEM?

Unless firm and immediate steps are taken to reverse the present trend, the public school system in the Northern cities of America will become predominantly a segregated system, serving primarily Negroes. It will, in addition, become a school system of low academic standards, providing a second-class education for underclassed children and thereby a chief contributor to the perpetuation of the "social dynamite" which is the cumulative pathology of the ghetto.

In Chicago, 37 per cent of the elementary schools (compared with 22 per cent in New York) and 18 per cent of the high schools (compared with 2 per cent in New York) are now segregated; 48.3 per cent of the pupils in Chicago are now Negro. In Cleveland, 60 per cent of the elementary schools and 58 per cent of the high schools are segregated, white or Negro. In Detroit, more than 40 per cent of public school children are Negro. In Philadelphia, more than half of the public school children are now Negro. By 1963 the Washington, D.C., public schools, which ten years ago had been one-third Negro, had become more than three-quarters Negro; by 1970, more than nine out of ten children in the public schools in the nation's capital may be Negro.

In the public schools of Manhattan as a whole, 73 per cent of the children are already nonwhites. Ninety per cent of school-age children in Harlem are in public schools; only two-thirds of the children in the rest of Manhattan are—the others have moved into private or parochial schools. Despite the fact that segregation has been illegal in the public school system of New York State since 1902, virtually all the 31,469 children in Harlem's schools (twenty elementary schools, four junior high schools, and no high schools) are Negro. Only two of the elementary schools have less than 89.9 per cent Negro enrollment; and all the junior high schools are at least 91.4 per cent Negro. This means that the bulk of the community's children in elementary and junior high schools are educated in *de facto* segregated schools although the city's Board of Education has an official policy of full integration.

The trend toward school segregation, in fact, is accelerating. Seventy-eight New York schools below high school became segregated between 1958 and 1963. Open enrollment and the free choice transfer policy, allowing parents to seek the transfer of their children to nonsegregated schools, have done little to improve the situation—less than 3 per cent of the nonwhite students moved to other schools. Many whites point to this apathy on the part of Negroes as evidence that Negro families in general prefer segregated neighborhood schools to unsegregated distant schools. *Any* parent prefers a neighborhood school, all things being equal and often when not all is equal, and no public school desegregation plan that demands voluntary individual decisions is ever accepted by the majority of Negro or white parents. Yet even if more students did transfer out of the ghetto few, if any, whites would move into the ghetto, and while the schools of the ghetto themselves would probably decline in population, they would remain segregated.

The pairing system, often called the Princeton Plan, which merges the populations of two nearby elementary schools, one predominantly Negro and the other predominantly white, also offers little chance of success in complex urban residential patterns and school systems. The New York City Board of Education proposed in 1964 that twenty-one such pairings be made. If all were introduced at once—though the board responded to further reflection and to community pressures by reducing the proposed twenty-one to four—segregation in the city would be reduced by only 1 per cent. If twenty schools a year were so paired, an unlikely move, the school system would still be one-quarter segregated in 1970. Sprawling, densely populated cities are not manageable, peaceful suburban communities like Princeton, and because the plan works in one area is no guarantee it will work in another.

In 1963, 45 per cent of New York's nonwhite children attended segregated junior highs. The Board of Education proposals to change the system of feeding students from elementary schools into junior highs would reduce this percentage only slightly. At this rate, and providing that the city's population did not itself change, the junior high schools of New York would be desegregated by about 2010. On the other hand, efforts to desegregate the twenty-five schools dominated now by nonwhites would make a difference in a single decade. If important efforts to achieve school integration are not adopted, segregation in the public schools will increase from 22 per cent of the elementary schools in 1963 to 38 per cent in 1975; from 19 to 29 per cent of the junior high schools; from 2 to 6 per cent of the high schools. The schools by 1980 would be three-quarters Negro and Puerto Rican in the city as a whole and in Manhattan would probably exceed 90 per cent, though the proportion may be expected to stabilize at that point.

One of the remedies suggested has been long-distance transportation of elementary school pupils, or "bussing." This plan seems to offer immediate desegregation, but in many cases it would lead to bad education and, in the end, therefore, to even more segregation. Whites would pull out of the public school system even more rapidly than they are presently doing. In Brooklyn, for example, if real integration were the goal, about 70,000 Negro and Puerto Rican children under eleven would have to be transported twice a day, some of them ten miles away. In Manhattan, where schools have an even higher proportion of Negro and Puerto Rican children, even longer travel time would fail to bring about meaningful integration. As the Allen Commission Report said:

> It should be obvious, but does not always appear to be, that integration is impossible without white pupils. No plan can be acceptable, therefore, which increases the movement of white pupils out of the public schools. Neither is it acceptable, however, unless it contributes to desegregation.

Therefore, any effective plan must (1) reduce school segregation; (2) bring better educational services; and (3) hold white pupils, even bring more back into the public school system.

One cannot help noting, however, that the interest in neighborhood schools, however valid, seems to have some relation to human hypocrisy. The white Parents and Taxpayers (PAT) groups in New York threatened boycotts over the school system's plan to transfer 383 children no more than a mile and a half for a ten-minute ride. Assistant Superintendent of Schools Jacob Landers noted that 77,000 children, including 25,000 in parochial schools, have been transferred regularly, and not for purposes of integration. The largest number were children in kindergarten and first and second grades, the same age group whose welfare is invoked fervently in behalf of the neighborhood school.

Many who have been themselves deeply damaged by past patterns of racial segregation will continue to resist the demands of the present. The demands of Negroes for desegregated schools will be met by many and continued forms of subtle and flagrant resistance. The school boycotts organized by civil rights groups in New York to force desegregation in the schools were rooted in the belief that such desegregation was immediately possible. But given the timidity and moral irresolution of whites, any such assumption is unrealistic, and the strategy doomed to fail. All white families need to do in event of forced desegregation is to form a counter-movement, as PAT did, and threaten to leave the community, as thousands have already done, or shift their children to private or parochial schools.

Whenever minority group membership in a community increases in the neighborhood of a public school, white families who can afford it tend to take their children out of public school and either move to a new community or send the children to the comparative safety of the private and parochial schools. The white protest groups that arrange community boycotts against integrated schools represent the marginal families who can neither move nor pay private school tuition. These groups react out of that despair which Negroes themselves often reflect when they see no alternatives in a threatening situation.

Less than 10 per cent of the private and parochial school population in New York is Negro—about 32,000 pupils; the 90 per cent who are white students represent 30 per cent of the city's white student population. So, while nine out of ten Negro children are in public schools, only seven out of ten white children are. An ironic possibility is that the present middle-class flight from the public schools which is explained in terms of the desire for quality education will not result in quality education at all. It is conceivable that with the proliferation of private and parochial schools in the urban areas, these schools will not be able to obtain the necessary finances and faculty for a truly quality education. They might then have to base their appeal only on status needs.

Most of New York City's private schools are parochial or church-sponsored, Roman Catholic and Episcopalian predominantly, with a few sponsored by Quakers, Jews, Ethical Culture societies, and others. Roman Catholic and certain Jewish schools give primary emphasis to the parents' desire to reinforce their children's religious loyalty. The Protestant and Ethical Culture groups, in particular, give quality of education as the chief reason for the existence of these private schools. But whatever the intent of the sponsors, many parents—some Negroes as well as whites—send their children to these schools not only for religious training or the sake of quality education but also to escape the growing influx of low-income minority group members into the public school system. There is a real question, of course, whether religion is best served by a displacement of a city's leadership into a private school system. There is a real question, also, whether socially insulated education *is* really education for leadership. The middle- and upper-class parents who defend their decision for private schools with the plea: "I won't sacrifice my child," give perhaps less weight to their children's resilience than the evidence would support, and certainly less weight to the importance of democratically based education than the times demand. But such arguments have little weight when parents fear for their child's future. In American life, where education is considered the first prerequisite for adult success, the issue is especially sensitive. When the question of education, therefore, is combined with the even more sensitive question of race, the emotions of persons are aroused as they seldom are by a public question.

EDUCATIONAL INEQUALITY

One thing is clear and that is that meaningful desegregation of urban ghetto public schools can occur only if all of the schools in the system are raised to the highest standards, so that the quality of education does not vary according to income or the social status of the neighborhood. The goals of integration and quality education must be sought together; they are interdependent. One is not possible without the other.

A number of individuals prominent in the civil rights movement claim, however, that a demand for excellence in ghetto schools is really camouflage for acquiescence in segregation. On the contrary it is, given the intransigence of the white community and the impossibility of immediate integration, a decision to save as many Negro children as possible now. The struggle of the civil rights groups for a better life for these children is made more difficult, if not impossible, if the methods of the struggle become dominated by inflexible emotional postures. Heroics and dramatic words and gestures, oversimplified either-or thinking, and devil-hunting might dominate headlines; but they cannot solve the fundamental problems of obtaining high-quality education in the public schools and the related problem of realistic and serious desegregation of these schools. These children, Negro or white, must not be sacrificed on the altars of ideological and semantic rigidities.

THE FIGHT FOR COMMUNITY CONTROL: P.S. 201 IN HARLEM

Many ghetto residents have come to the conclusion that they can never obtain decent schools for their children as long as control is in the hands of remote officials. This selection describes the attempt of some parents in Harlem to gain control over a new intermediate school.

From Nat Hentoff, "Making Public Schools Accountable: A Case Study of P.S. 201 in Harlem," Phi Delta Kappan *48, No. 7 (March, 1967): 332–35. Reprinted by permission of Phi Delta Kappan, Inc., and Nat Hentoff.*

Consider yourself a parent of a child in a ghetto school in any large city in America. You know—from television, from the unemployed standing useless in the streets of your ghetto every day—that your child is growing into a society in which the quality of his education will be crucial to what becomes of him.

Consider yourself a parent of a child in Harlem. This year, nearly 85 per cent of all sixth-grade children in Harlem are two years or more below the city-wide average in reading achievement. Two-thirds of the Harlem children who go on to high school this year will drop out.

Kenneth Clark, the Negro psychologist who has spent years trying to convince the educational establishment to share his and Harlem's parents' acute urgency concerning this waste of children, now says:

> It is not necessary for even the most prejudiced personnel officer to discriminate against Negro youth, because the schools have done the job for them. The massively gross inefficiency of the public schools has so limited the occupational possibilities of the Negro youth that, if not mandatory, a life of menial status or employment is virtually inevitable.

As a parent of a child caught in this quicksand, what would you do? This year, one group of parents in East Harlem, desperate for their children, decided to act. A new intermediate school, I.S. 201 (for grades five to eight) was about to open. From 1958 on, parents and other community groups had protested to the Board of Education that the site for the new school would insure it being a segregated school. No, said the board, steps will be taken to make the new school a model of "quality, integrated" education.

The board lied. In the spring of 1966, the local superintendent had the stunning gall to tell the parents that a way had indeed been found to integrate I.S. 201: It would be 50 per cent Negro and 50 per cent Puerto Rican. But, the board tried to calm the outraged parents, look at all the money we've put into I.S. 201. It cost a million dollars more than others of the same size. It's air-conditioned.

The parents looked at the school, standing on stilts, with no windows facing into the streets. And many of them, as one observer put it, regarded its design "as a symbol of the city's attitude toward this impoverished area, the windowless façade standing for an averted eye."

Parent opposition prevented the school opening in April. During the summer, a plan began to be formulated by groups in the community. Among those who shaped it was Preston Wilcox, a professor of community organization at Columbia's School of Social Work. Wilcox, a Negro, had long been involved in community action groups outside the classroom. The essence of the plan, as Wilcox described it in *The Urban Review* (a publication of the Center for Urban Education) was the establishment of a school-community committee. "It would be composed," he wrote, "of individuals with close ties to, and knowledge of, the community. These individuals would be parents, local leaders and professionals in educational or social science fields who would be drawn from the community or outside it, if necessary."

The committee, which would screen and interview candidates for principal of the school,

> would have access to all reports sent by school administrators to the district supervisor and the Board of Education, and it would be empowered to hold open meetings to which parents and teachers would be invited to present their suggestions or complaints. Additionally, it would have the responsibility of providing a continuous review of the curriculum to ensure that it remains relevant to the needs and experience of the students and that it be sufficiently demanding to bring out their best possible performances.

There were other provisions in the plan, but its core was the possibility that this experimental program would provide that "in at least one school in one community the school administrator and teachers would be made accountable to the community, and the community made obliged to them. . . ."

The Board of Education, still pointing to the splendor of the building, ignored the plan until threat of a boycott brought the superintendent of schools and the president of the Board of Education to East Harlem to negotiate with the parents. Surprisingly, the emissaries from the establishment agreed to the formation of a community council which would, among other responsibilities, help select new personnel—including teachers—and make recommendations and evaluations of the curriculum.

The parents also wanted a Negro principal. The basic reason, as pointed out in a letter to the *New York Times* by L. Alexander Harper (director for school and community integration, United Church of Christ), was that "when the school administrator becomes the prime daily adult male authority image for children needing racial self-respect and ambition, the race of that principal may prove an educational factor more important than we prefer to believe."

At one point, the Board of Education seemed about to accept this parent demand too. By a behind-the-scenes application of official pressure, Lisser was made to "voluntarily resign"; his place was to be taken temporarily by a Negro assistant principal, Miss Beryl Banfield. She refused. Significantly, only part of the reason for her refusal was carried by the white press, including the *New York Times*. She said—and was cheered by white editorial writers for saying it—that she wanted to be selected on merit and not on race.

But the Negro weekly, the *New York Amsterdam News*, carried a more complete and more revealing statement by Miss Banfield:

The offer for me to be acting principal of this school was a fraudulent one. Not having a principal's license, I know I could not command the full stature and respect of that position. If I had accepted it, it would have been a disservice to the community, the school, and myself. If I had taken the position of acting principal in this school, it would have helped shield the fact that the Board of Education had no Negro principal immediately available on the list to offer the job to. Therefore, I would have been an instrument for covering up a serious lack on the part of the Board of Education. So, I chose to decline. [There are only four Negro principals out of 870 in the New York City public school system.]

In any case, the board withdrew its offer to appoint a black head of the school. Counterpressures from an organization of principals had shaken the board; and then it collapsed when the 55 teachers in the school (26 of them Negro) said they would not work unless Lisser was returned. The position of the teachers in I.S. 201 was understandable. They were afraid that community involvement in I.S. 201 could transcend their rights under the tenure provisions of the United Federation of Teachers' contract with the board. And, of course, the UFT supported its teachers. The teachers and most others involved were too panicky to hear what the parents were saying—that they did not intend to violate teachers' tenure rights in the school system as a whole but did want to have a chance to participate in the interviewing of new teachers for *their* school.

A boycott resulted, and there were turbulent days of picketing and police lines. The most empathetic of all the accounts of the boycott in the daily press was that of Earl Caldwell in the *New York Post:* "The parents have many allies now," he wrote, "and they run the gamut of the Harlem community. It's more than just a group of parents fighting for something they call 'quality education.' It's a community now that feels it must overturn a system that is working against it."

The boycott faded, but parental unrest remained high. Kenneth Clark decided to propose a new plan: attaching I.S. 201 to a university and then removing this partnership from the Board of Education's control by delegating authority to a private operational board. The parents' committee of I.S. 201, as Andrew Kopkind reported in an excellent summary of the situation in the October 22, 1966, *New Republic,*

took Clark's suggestion and grafted on it a measure of "community control" from the now-deferred Wilcox proposal. It was far from the "total" control they had demanded, and many of the more militant protesters were peeved at the compromise, but the group decided it was worth a try. Clark was the broker between the committee and the school board. He shuffled between meetings of the one in Harlem, and the other in Brooklyn, and was almost destroyed in the crossfire. In his account, the board was duplicitous, discourteous, and unresponsive. The parents were suspicious and demanding. He finally decided to bow out, after a long session with the school board. When it was over, he later told the parents frankly, "I went home and cried. I don't believe the board is serious or takes the people of this community seriously," he said. "The time has come for people themselves to return to direct dealing with the board."

As of this writing, there has been no communication between the parents and the board for months. The mayor of New York, John Lindsay, has tried to move the board at least to prepare itself for such future confrontations by instructing it to appoint a task force of "prominent citizens" to explore the problems of ghetto schools and recommend basic changes. McGeorge Bundy of the Ford Foundation is reportedly willing to head such a task force, but so far no Negro whom people in Harlem would trust has agreed to serve on the task force. There have been too many committees, too many studies.

As for I.S. 201, on January 23, 1967, the *New York Times* reported that

the "showcase" school . . . has a wary principal facing a still-hostile community. Many of its teachers feel encircled by tension and without support and its pupils are often defiant and undisciplined. . . . While unruliness is a common problem at many schools, it is so persistent at this "model" school that in many classes the chatter of even two or three students has sent teachers into rages.

The board meanwhile, having promised so much to this school, has forgotten it. A science teacher, waving a 26-page list of supplies he had been trying to get for months, told the *Time's* reporter: "The parents were right. As soon as you open the school, the system forgets about you." Several teachers have resigned and more are planning to do so.

There will almost certainly be renewed pressure from the community to force some degree of meaningful local participation in I.S. 201 before it slides irretrievably into being just another ghetto school. Meanwhile, parents in other ghetto neighborhoods in New York, in Rochester, in other cities, are beginning to organize themselves to find ways in which the school system and particular principals can be made *accountable*.

Obviously, it's too soon to tell, but the revolt at I.S. 201 may turn out to have been the start of radical restructuring of school-community relations in many other places besides ghettos. And its impact may go beyond education. As *New Left Notes*, a publication of Students for a Democratic Society, points out:

When the parents talk of control and participating they bring out a demand which is relevant for the entire society concerning every social institution. Their demands form the seed of the general call for the origination of alternative structures to the prevalent power relationships in American society. Community control in primary education is analogous to student-faculty control in the university and one step from popular democratic control over all the public institutions that . . . affect us.

Youthful overoptimism? Alas, probably it is. But who knows? The ghettos may yet have something to teach us all about making democracy a participatory experience. It may be, as Preston Wilcox hopes, that "a community can organize effectively around the process of educating its children." And once organized, it can move to effect other basic changes in the way its members live and work.

Back at I.S. 201, a reporter for the *New Yorker* interviewed principal Stanley Lisser soon after the *visible* protests from the community had temporarily subsided. What had he learned from the experience? "I am proud of the children of this community," he said. "The way they rose to this occasion indicates that we have been maligning both the children of the ghettos and their schools." It is a statement of such obtuseness and such smug ignorance that if I were a parent in that community, I would make the removal of Mr. Lisser from the school a primary life goal. Not because he's white, but because he clearly doesn't *belong* there.

He is "proud of the children of this community." But after they go through his school, will *they* be proud of the community? Black consciousness is rising, and one of its goals is the instillation of pride in the Negro young. As an organizer in East Harlem told reporter Andrew Kopkind, "the parents' concern is that whoever gets an education here will want to rebuild their community. Now, the most talented students leave. Only the dropouts stay. The only way I know to give young people the desire to return to Harlem—to stay in Harlem—is to let them be proud of Harlem."

Is this new school, with no windows facing into the streets, going to be able to let them be proud of Harlem? Not as it is now.

V A Way of Life

Although the city was looked upon as a place of hope by many migrants, Negroes found that their opportunities for personal fulfillment were blocked in innumerable ways that whites seemed incapable of comprehending. At the same time the coming together of large numbers of blacks created a milieu that encouraged the development of a new and positive racial consciousness and an impressive creative outpouring. The most exciting example was probably that associated with the work of the writers, artists, and musicians of the Harlem Renaissance of the 1920s. In this section, both these negative and positive aspects of the city are illustrated.

If the city helped to release creative energies, it also strained many of the older institutions of Negro life. This was certainly true for the church and family, which played vital roles in providing needed stability in the impersonal and hostile urban environment. This section continues with selections discussing changes and problems concerning both of these institutions.

1 THE NEW NEGRO

*The growth of an urban Negro population was accompanied by the
emergence of numerous new, articulate, and often aggressive leaders and
organizations. Many, like W. E. B. DuBois, rejected the accommodations
accepted by Booker T. Washington, whose death in 1915 removed the
most important of the older leaders. Central themes of the spirit of the
"New Negro" were racial pride and independence. In 1925 Alain
Locke, a Rhodes scholar, Harvard Ph.D., and author, edited a special
issue of* The Survey *magazine devoted to Harlem, which was an
impressive statement of the accomplishments of many of the new Negroes.
This selection is from Locke's introductory essay.*

From Alain Locke, "Enter the New Negro," The Survey *53, No. 11
(March 1, 1925): 631–34.*

In the last decade something beyond the watch and guard of statistic
has happened in the life of the American Negro and the three norns wh
have traditionally presided over the Negro problem have a changelir
in their laps. The Sociologist, The Philanthropist, the Race-leader ar
not unaware of the New Negro, but they are at a loss to account for hin
He simply cannot be swathed in their formulae. For the younger genera
tion is vibrant with a new psychology; the new spirit is awake in th
masses, and under the very eyes of the professional observers is trans
forming what has been a perennial problem into the progressive phase
of contemporary Negro life.

Could such a metamorphosis have taken place as suddenly as it ha
appeared to? The answer is no; not because the New Negro is not here
but because the Old Negro had long become more of a myth than a mar
The Old Negro, we must remember, was a creature of moral debate an
historical controversy. His has been a stock figure perpetuated as a
historical fiction partly in innocent sentimentalism, partly in deliberat
reactionism. The Negro himself has contributed his share to this throug
a sort of protective social mimicry forced upon him by the adverse circum
stances of dependence. So for generations in the mind of America, th
Negro has been more of a formula than a human being—a somethin
to be argued about, condemned or defended, to be "kept down," o

"in his place," or "helped up," to be worried with or worried over, harassed or patronized, a social bogey or a social burden. The thinking Negro even has been induced to share this same general attitude, to focus his attention on controversial issues, to see himself in the distorted perspective of a social problem. His shadow, so to speak, has been more real to him than his personality. Through having had to appeal from the unjust stereotypes of his oppressors and traducers to those of his liberators, friends and benefactors he has subscribed to the traditional positions from which his case has been viewed. Little true social or self-understanding has or could come from such a situation. . . .

With this renewed self-respect and self-dependence, the life of the Negro community is bound to enter a new dynamic phase, the buoyancy from within compensating for whatever pressure there may be of conditions from without. The migrant masses, shifting from countryside to city, hurdle several generations of experience at a leap, but more important, the same thing happens spiritually in the life-attitudes and self-expression of the Young Negro, in his poetry, his art, his education and his new outlook, with the additional advantage, of course, of the poise and greater certainty of knowing what it is all about. From this comes the promise and warrant of a new leadership. . . . The day of "aunties," "uncles" and "mammies" is equally gone. Uncle Tom and Sambo have passed on, and even the "Colonel" and "George" play barnstorm roles from which they escape with relief when the public spotlight is off. The popular melodrama has about played itself out, and it is time to scrap the fictions, garret the bogeys and settle down to a realistic facing of facts.

First we must observe some of the changes which since the traditional lines of opinion were drawn have rendered these quite obsolete. A main change has been, of course, that shifting of the Negro population which has made the Negro problem no longer exclusively or even predominantly Southern. Why should our minds remain sectionalized, when the problem itself no longer is? Then the trend of migration has not only been toward the North and the Central Midwest, but city-ward and to the great centers of industry—the problems of adjustment are new, practical, local and not peculiarly racial. Rather they are an integral part of the large industrial and social problems of our present-day democracy. And finally, with the Negro rapidly in [the] process of class differentiation, if it ever was warrantable to regard and treat the Negro en masse it is becoming with every day less possible, more unjust and more ridiculous.

The Negro too, for his part, has idols of the tribe to smash. If on the one hand the white man has erred in making the Negro appear to be that which would excuse or extenuate his treatment of him, the Negro, in turn, has too often unnecessarily excused himself because of the way he has been treated. The intelligent Negro of today is resolved not to make discrimination an extenuation for his shortcomings in performance, in-dividual or collective; he is trying to hold himself at par, neither inflated by sentimental allowances nor deprecated by current social discounts. . . .

It does not follow that if the Negro were better known, he would be better liked or better treated. But mutual understanding is basic for any subsequent cooperation and adjustment. The effort toward this will at least have the effect of remedying in large part what has been the most unsatisfactory feature of our present stage of race relationships in America, namely the fact that the more intelligent and representative elements of the two race groups have at so many points got quite out of vital touch with one another. . . .

. . . In the intellectual realm a renewed and keen curiosity is replacing the recent apathy; the Negro is being carefully studied, not just talked about and discussed. In arts and letters, instead of being wholly carica-tured, he is being seriously portrayed and painted.

To all of this the New Negro is keenly responsive as an augury of a new democracy in American culture. He is contributing his share to the new social understanding. But the desire to be understood would never in itself have been sufficient to have opened so completely the protectively closed portals of the thinking Negro's mind. There is still too much pos-sibility of being snubbed or patronized for that. It was rather the necessity for fuller, truer self-expression, the realization of the unwisdom of allowing social discrimination to segregate him mentally, and a counter-attitude to cramp and fetter his own living—and so the "spite-wall" that the intellectuals built over the "color-line" has happily been taken down. Much of this reopening of intellectual contacts has centered in New York and has been richly fruitful not merely in the enlarging of personal ex-perience, but in the definite enrichment of American arts and letters and in the clarifying of our common vision of the social tasks ahead. . . .

Each generation, however, will have its creed and that of the present is the belief in the efficacy of collective effort, in race cooperation. This deep feeling of race is at present the mainspring of Negro life. It seems to be the outcome of the reaction to proscription and prejudice, an attempt, fairly successful on the whole, to convert a defensive into an offensive position, a handicap into an incentive. It is radical in tone, but not in purpose and only the most stupid forms of opposition, misunder-standing or persecution could make it otherwise. Of course, the thinking Negro has shifted a little toward the left with the world trend, and there is an increasing group who affiliate with radical and liberal movements. But fundamentally for the present the Negro is radical on race matters, conservative on others, in other words, a "forced radical," a social protestant rather than a genuine radical. Yet under further pressure and injustice iconoclastic thought and motives will inevitably increase. Harlem's quixotic radicalisms call for their ounce of democracy today lest tomorrow they be beyond cure.

The Negro mind reaches out as yet to nothing but American wants, American ideas. But this forced attempt to build his Americanism on race values is a unique social experiment, and its ultimate success is impossible except through the fullest sharing of American culture and institutions. There should be no delusion about this. American nerves in sections unstrung with race hysteria are often fed the opiate that the trend of Negro advance is wholly separatist, and that the effect of its operation will be to encyst the Negro as a benign foreign body in the body politic. This cannot be—even if it were desirable. The racialism of the Negro is no limitation or reservation with respect to American life; it is only a constructive effort to build the obstructions in the stream of his progress into an efficient dam of social energy and power. Democracy itself is obstructed and stagnated to the extent that any of its channels are closed. Indeed they cannot be selectively closed. So the choice is not between one way for the Negro and another way for the rest, but between American institutions frustrated on the one hand and American ideals progressively fulfilled and realized on the other. . . .

Fortunately there are constructive channels opening out into which the balked social feelings of the American Negro can flow freely. Without them there would be much more pressure and danger than there is. These compensating interests are racial but in a new and enlarged way. One is the consciousness of acting as the advance guard of the African peoples in their contact with twentieth century civilization; the other, the sense of a mission of rehabilitating the race in world esteem from that loss of prestige for which the fate and conditions of slavery have so largely been responsible. Harlem, as we shall see, is the center of both these movements; she is the home of the Negro's "Zionism." The pulse of the Negro world has begun to beat in Harlem. A Negro newspaper carrying news material in English, French and Spanish, gathered from all quarters of America, the West Indies and Africa has maintained itself in Harlem for over five years. Two important magazines, both edited [in] New York, maintain their news and circulation consistently on a cosmopolitan scale. Under American auspices and backing, three pan-African congresses have been held abroad for the discussion of common interests, colonial questions and the future cooperative development of Africa. In terms of the race question as a world problem, the Negro mind has leapt, so to speak, upon the parapets of prejudice and extended its cramped horizons. In so doing it has linked up with the growing group consciousness of the dark peoples and is gradually learning their common interests. As one of our writers has recently put it: "It is imperative that

we understand the white world in its relations to the nonwhite world."
As with the Jew, persecution is making the Negro international.

As a world phenomenon this wider race consciousness is a different
thing from the much asserted rising tide of color. Its inevitable causes are
not of our making. The consequences are not necessarily damaging to the
best interests of civilization. Whether it actually brings into being new
Armadas of conflict or argosies of cultural exchange and enlightenment
can only be decided by the attitude of the dominant races in an era of
critical change. With the American Negro his new internationalism is
primarily an effort to recapture contact with the scattered peoples of
African derivation. Garveyism may be a transient, if spectacular, phenomenon, but the possible role of the American Negro in the future
development of Africa is one of the most constructive and universally
helpful missions that any modern people can lay claim to.

Constructive participation in such causes cannot help giving the Negro
valuable group incentives, as well as increased prestige at home and
abroad. Our greatest rehabilitation may possibly come through such
channels, but for the present, more immediate hope rests in the revalua-
tion by white and black alike of the Negro in terms of his artistic endow-
ments and cultural contributions, past and prospective. It must be
increasingly recognized that the Negro has already made very substantial
contributions, not only in his folk-art, music especially, which has always
found appreciation, but in larger, though humbler and less acknowledged
ways. For generations the Negro has been the peasant matrix of that
section of America which has most undervalued him, and here he has
contributed not only materially in labor and in social patience, but
spiritually as well. The South has unconsciously absorbed the gift of his
folk temperament. In less than half a generation it will be easier to recognize this, but the fact remains that a leaven of humor, sentiment, imagination and tropic nonchalance has gone into the making of the South from a
humble, unacknowledged source. A second crop of the Negro's gifts
promises still more. . . . He now becomes a conscious contributor and
lays aside the status of a beneficiary and ward for that of a collaborator
and participant in American civilization. The great social gain in this is
the releasing of our talented group from the arid fields of controversy
and debate to the productive fields of creative expression. The especially
cultural recognition they win should in turn prove the key to that re-
valuation of the Negro which must precede or accompany any considerable further betterment of race relationships. But whatever the general
effect, the present generation will have added the motives of self-expression
and spiritual development to the old and still unfinished task of making
material headway and progress. No one who understandingly faces the
situation with its substantial accomplishment or views the new scene with
its still more abundant promise can be entirely without hope. And

certainly, if in our lifetime the Negro should not be able to celebrate his full initiation into American democracy, he can at least, on the warrant of these things, celebrate the attainment of a significant and satisfying new phase of group development, and with it a spiritual Coming of Age.

2 CLAUDE BROWN SURVIVES THE HARLEM GHETTO

For many blacks, life in the big-city ghetto was vastly different from the experience of the "New Negro" artists and intellectuals of the 1920s. In this selection, Claude Brown graphically depicts his own struggle for survival in the Harlem of the 1940s and early 1950s. Despite the hardships and brutality that he faced during these years, Brown did not succumb to the urban jungle, and in his autobiography, Manchild in the Promised Land, *published in 1965, he showed impressive talent as a writer.*

From Claude Brown, "Harlem, My Harlem," Dissent 8, *No. 3 (Summer, 1961): 378–82. Reprinted by permission of Dissent Publishing Corporation.*

At the age of nine I had already acquired the reputation of being the worst boy in the neighborhood. And in my neighborhood this was no easy accomplishment. My frequent appearance in juvenile court was beginning to bother the judges. By spring of 1946 I had been placed in four juvenile detention centers by the Manhattan Domestic Relations Court. However, during my travels through New York City while truant from school, I had become exceptionally well acquainted with the city subways. As a result, I was usually back on the streets of Harlem within two days, from wherever the court had placed me. A year earlier, I had acquired the habit of staying away from home for several days and nights which occasionally lengthened into weeks. Due to my skill at living in the streets, it would sometimes be many days before my parents learned of my unofficial departure from the places to which I had been confined by the courts.

While roaming the streets at night with one or two other boys who were also afraid to go home or disgusted with home life, I was often arrested for breaking into stores and stealing. I only stole items that I could sell to my private customers or to one of the neighborhood "fences." And I knew a large number of the latter. Among my many customers and associates were prostitutes, pimps, dope peddlers, stick-up artists, professional thieves, and other petty criminals with great ambitions.

My favorite fence was Miss Eileen. She was not the highest paying fence; in fact, there is no such thing. Any thief will tell you, they are all a bunch of crooks. But Miss Eileen had such a nice way of robbing me. She would put her arm around me and beg me in a very sexy tone while she played with my ears. I thought she was the prettiest lady in the world. I think she was the first woman I ever knew who had red hair. Miss Eileen was also something more than a fence, and I would have discovered this much sooner had it not been for my youth. Many times when I came to her house at night she would be in her slip and a new husband would be there. As time went on I heard the older fellows talking about selling Miss Eileen something for a "piece of loving." I too began to dream of the day when I could sell her something for a piece of loving, but to my regret I never got the chance. A year later Miss Eileen went to jail for three years, and when she came out she wasn't as pretty as she used to be. As a result, she changed her "game" to selling drugs. For three years she was very successful in the "horse trade," but gave it up and did seven years for her troubles at the insistence of the Narcotics Bureau. The last time I saw her she was profitably engaged in one of Harlem's more legal vices; the "numbers" racket.

These were the people I admired and wanted to be accepted by. People like Miss Eileen and my other teachers from the streets of Harlem.

By June 1946 I had been expelled from not less than six public schools in New York City, and refused acceptance by as many others. The Board of Education would tolerate my numerous absences from school, and even my fighting with teachers. But they refused to have a boy in the school system who had attempted to push another boy out of a five-story window.

Following a thirty-day psychiatric observation period in Bellevue Hospital, I was ordered out of the state by a juvenile court judge. After enduring what seemed at the time a miserable year on a small farm in South Carolina, I returned to New York. When I arrived in Harlem on August 10, 1947 I was also returning to a familiar way of life. Less than two months later I was standing before Judge Bolyn diligently trying to look pathetic. She appeared to be a woman devoid of any emotions, especially pity. From Judge Bolyn, to whom I am deeply indebted today, I received my first sentence.

My first court sentence was actually not a sentence at all, but a commitment to Wiltwyck School for Boys for an indefinite time.

Wiltwyck is an interracial institution which accepts delinquent boys from eight to twelve, committed by the courts of New York or by social agencies. Only children are considered who can profit by its program of individualized treatment in the regulated and planned environment of a children's community.

Following a two-and-a-half-years stay at Wiltwyck, I returned to my dear old Harlem. I was then thirteen. In a few weeks I became uncomfortably aware of not being able to fit in anymore. There were many new vices to learn, but somehow I just could not pick up where I had left off. Having no alternative, however, I set out to reestablish myself in the old community.

Things were somewhat different now. The dope fad had hit New York, and all of my old gang were using heroin. I wanted nothing to do with drugs, but the problem was very disturbing. Either I could continue my relationship with my old cohorts or get in with a younger gang of delinquents, my own age. The younger group was stealing and making much less money than my former partners. I would have chosen my old friends, but I was handicapped by parental restrictions. So I became leader of a gang of fellows mostly my own age. There were many things I could teach them, such as how to pick locks, how to rob a subway slot machine, how to pick a woman's pocketbook, how to bargain with the "fence," and how to roll "pot." Also, I knew how to organize a gang fight and hold a gang together.

I didn't have to steal for money, because Butch, Kidd, and Danny were doing good, "pushing horse," and money was mine for the asking. I think they preferred that I steal it from them. So, that's how I usually got it. Butch, Kidd, and Danny were all at least four years older than I was, and for many years we had all lived in the same tenement building. These guys whom I considered to be "big time," were like older brothers to me. They fought the bigger guys who tried to bully me. It was they who had taught me how to steal, how to live in the streets of Harlem. It was Danny who had taught me most of the street ways. He taught me by cheating me, taking me along on "scores," and showing me my mistakes whenever I lost a fight.

Whenever I lost a fight Danny would always say you should have stabbed that punk. To Danny, everybody was a punk. It was Danny who had first taught me how to use a knife in a street fight. I remember him showing me how to get the knife out of my belt without my opponent seeing it. Danny would say "a cat should never know that you have a knife until he has been cut or stabbed." And this is usually the way it was when he stabbed a guy.

Butch was the most loyal guy I knew, and also the best thief. Butch had taught me how to hitch rides on street cars and buses. He also taught me not to run when I stole something. Butch would never admit that he was the best thief in the neighborhood. He would always say that Sol was the best because Sol had taught him many things about stealing. Sol was much older than Butch and had been stealing much longer, but he had been caught while Butch had not yet been "busted." In my opinion that made Butch the better thief.

Kidd had taught me how to play hookey from school. I was about six years old when I first heard about "hookey" and I pleaded with Kidd to teach me the game. He promised me he would teach me on the first day I went to school. This promise had to wait until the second day, because on the first day my mother took me to get me registered. Once I learned how to play hookey, I seldom went to school, and this often led to staying away from home. I would look in the mailbox and could always tell if there was a card from the school. The yellow truancy card in the mailbox meant that if I went home that night, the razor strop awaited me. When I played hookey I would either go on a stealing tour of the city or sneak into a movie. Kidd had also taught me how to sneak into a movie.

Stealing had become a part of me and I became very adept at this art. After Wiltwyck I felt lost whenever I was not stealing or "rumbling." Perhaps that's why I began to spend more time with my new gang and less time with my old cohorts.

Less than three months after my release, I was arrested for gang fighting, but was released in my mother's custody. Three weeks later I was in a backyard stealing some sheets off a clothes line. Turk, a member of my new gang whom I had become "tight" with, was with me. At my house there were festivities taking place because mama had hit the number. I had to get away from it and when I reached the street, the first person I saw was Turk. He was always ready to do whatever I suggested. Turk's favorite words were "Sonny, what are we gonna do?" That cold night in December, when I said to Turk, let's go steal some sheets, he seemed to be waiting for the suggestion.

When we had been in the backyard for about fifteen minutes, Turk shouted, "Foot it, Sonny!" I stood there waiting to see what he wanted to run from. I didn't see anybody, but after the first shot was fired I decided to run. By the time I reached the top of the stairs leading from the backyard I was feeling unusually tired. But I kept running even after I felt the blood streaming down my leg and realized I had been shot. I panicked and started yelling, "Turk! Turk! I'm shot." I ran into a fish-and-chip joint where I collapsed. As I lay on the floor of the dirty joint, my fear of dying began slowly to diminish.

I found myself wishing that mama would stop jumping up while she cried, because she was shaking the shabby floor and it made me feel the bullet more. I never gave a second thought to Turk's question when he bent over me as I fell to the floor, and asked me if I were going to tell the cops that he was with me. This was all very normal in Harlem where somebody was always getting shot, stabbed, or his throat cut. However, I found it disturbing to have it happen to me. As the pain began to ease up, I started thinking how lucky I was to die this way. I thought about the boy whom I had watched two members of my old gang throw from the roof of a six-story building. I recalled how frightened he looked when they grabbed him, and I recalled his terrified screams as he went over. Yeah, compared to him I was really lucky.

While I lay on the rolling stretcher in Harlem Hospital emergency ward, I thought the police would never stop questioning me. Danny, Butch, and Kidd arrived shortly after I did. First Butch would beg me to tell him who had shot me, then Danny would start while Kidd threatened to kill Turk if I died. They all had their "pieces" and were ready and anxious to shoot somebody. Fortunately, I had not seen whoever it was that shot me, and could tell them no more than I had told the police.

Three weeks after my two-week stay in Harlem Hospital, and while the surgeon who had operated on me was still marveling at what he and God had done, I was sent to New York State Training School for Boys at Warwick, New York. I stayed at Warwick for nine months. When I returned to Harlem, I had learned many new ways of crimes. I had also become well acquainted with many of New York City's teenage criminals.

Upon my return to Harlem I no longer cared to steal or partake in gang fights, but I had to steal a few things to show my gang that getting shot had not unnerved me. Two days after I came home, I received my first real pistol, as a coming home gift. After pulling enough scores to get up one hundred dollars, I bought a half pound of pot and went into business. Within two weeks, the word had gotten around that I had the best pot in town. For the next three months—at the end of which I got "busted"—I did a pretty good job of emulating a Harlem "hustler" who was doing good. This included wearing thirty-dollar shoes and giving frequent handouts to old friends who had become junkies. Danny, one of my favorite old tutors in the ways of the street, had now become my favorite junkie; I would always give him a "nickel bill" to get a fix.

Following two more trips to Warwick, I moved out of Harlem and got a job. Most of my spare time was spent in Harlem, taking the ribbing and laughing that my attending evening high school evoked from my old street corner cronies. They laughed for three years. When I entered college there were no more laughs.

Some interesting changes have occurred in Harlem during the past few years. It seems that many of the people who I once thought were merely waiting for something to happen to them, have made things happen. The last time I saw Danny, I could not help but admire him. Danny is making

money by the fists full. There is nothing remarkable about a guy making lots of money selling drugs. But in Danny's case the admirable feat was
his being able to kick an eight-year drug habit, and then make the stuff
work for him. Danny is the only reformed junkie I have ever known to
stay reformed for any length of time. And his presence in Harlem is most
encouraging to other junkies who dream of kicking their habit and becoming pushers in turn.

I saw Turk yesterday and we talked of his next fight. It was an inspiring
experience for me to hear Turk, who has become one of the world's
leading heavyweight fighters, explain how he would beat his next opponent. It seems like only yesterday when I was explaining to him the
strategy of our next "rumble."

The big changes in Harlem are in the people I know who have changed
my sympathy to respect and admiration. If you've ever known a junkie
for any length of time you'll understand the struggle he has to go through
to get off the poison kick. He can't leave the world entirely, so for him to
become master and dispenser of the thing that had ruled him for so long
and so destructively is a great achievement. Harlem still has a much
greater number of the miserable than any place else I know. This is
inspiring also. Where else can one find so many people in such pain and
so few crying about it?

3   THE NEGRO CHURCH IN PHILADELPHIA

*In the city the church's function was different, and often less central to the
lives of Negroes, from what it had been in the rural South. Inevitably,
its concern with the secular problems of the urban community grew at the
expense of its strictly spiritual aspects. The individual churches in the
city were much larger than any in the South, and the successful ones
were run in an efficient, businesslike manner. In the Philadelphia of the
1890s, the Methodist church was the most important denomination,
followed by the Baptist. This selection describes the function of the
Negro Church at that time.*

From W. E. B. DuBois, The Philadelphia Negro: A Social Study
(Philadelphia: The University of Pennsylvania Press, 1899), pp. 201–6.

The Negro church is the peculiar and characteristic product of the transplanted African, and deserves especial study. As a social group the Negro church may be said to have antedated the Negro family on American soil; as such it has preserved, on the one hand, many functions of tribal organization, and on the other hand, many of the family functions. Its tribal functions are shown in its religious activity, its social authority and general guiding and coordinating work; its family functions are shown by the fact that the church is a centre of social life and intercourse; acts as newspaper and intelligence bureau; is the centre of amusements—indeed, is the world in which the Negro moves and acts. So far-reaching are these functions of the church that its organization is almost political. In Bethel Church, for instance, the mother African Methodist Episcopal Church of America, we have the following officials and organizations:

The Bishop of the District	
The Presiding Elder	Executive
The Pastor	
The Board of Trustees	Executive Council
General Church Meeting	Legislative
The Board of Stewards	
The Board of Stewardesses	Financial Board
The Junior Stewardesses	
The Sunday School Organization	Educational System
Ladies' Auxiliary, Volunteer Guild, etc.	Tax Collectors
Ushers' Association	Police
Class Leaders	
Local Preachers	Sheriffs and Magistrates
Choir	Music and Amusement
Allen Guards	Militia
Missionary Societies	Social Reformers
Beneficial and Semi-Secret Societies, etc.	Corporations

Or to put it differently, here we have a mayor, appointed from without, with great administrative and legislative powers, although well-limited by long and zealously cherished custom; he acts conjointly with a select council, the trustees, a board of finance, composed of stewards and stewardesses, a common council of committees and, occasionally, of all church members. The various functions of the church are carried out by societies and organizations. The form of government varies, but is generally some form of democracy closely guarded by custom and tempered by possible and not infrequent secession.

The functions of such churches in order of present emphasis are:

1. The raising of the annual budget
2. The maintenance of membership
3. Social intercourse and amusements

4. The setting of moral standards
5. Promotion of general intelligence
6. Efforts for social betterment . . .

Without wholly conscious effort the Negro church has become a centre of social intercourse to a degree unknown in white churches even in the country. The various churches, too, represent social classes. At St. Thomas' one looks for the well-to-do Philadelphians, largely descendants of favorite mulatto house-servants, and consequently well-bred and educated, but rather cold and reserved to strangers or newcomers; at Central Presbyterian one sees the older, simpler set of respectable Philadelphians with distinctly Quaker characteristics—pleasant but conservative; at Bethel may be seen the best of the great laboring class—steady, honest people, well dressed and well fed, with church and family traditions; at Wesley will be found the new arrivals, the sight-seers and the strangers to the city—hearty and easy-going people, who welcome all comers and ask few questions; at Union Baptist one may look for the Virginia servant girls and their young men; and so on throughout the city. Each church forms its own social circle, and not many stray beyond its bounds. Introductions into that circle come through the church, and thus the stranger becomes known. All sorts of entertainments and amusements are furnished by the churches: concerts, suppers, socials, fairs, literary exercises and debates, cantatas, plays, excursions, picnics, surprise parties, celebrations. Every holiday is the occasion of some special entertainment by some club, society or committee of the church; Thursday afternoons and evenings, when the servant girls are free, are always sure to have some sort of entertainment. Sometimes these exercises are free, sometimes an admission fee is charged, sometimes refreshments or articles are on sale. The favorite entertainment is a concert with solo singing, instrumental music, reciting and the like. Many performers make a living by appearing at these entertainments in various cities, and often they are persons of training and ability, although not always. So frequent are these and other church exercises that there are few Negro churches which are not open four to seven nights in a week and sometimes one or two afternoons in addition.

Perhaps the pleasantest and most interesting social intercourse takes place on Sunday; the weary week's work is done, the people have slept late and had a good breakfast, and sally forth to church well dressed and complacent. The usual hour of the morning service is eleven, but people stream in until after twelve. The sermon is usually short and stirring, but in the larger churches elicits little response other than an "Amen" or two. After the sermon the social features begin; notices on the various meetings of the week are read, people talk with each other in subdued tones, take their contributions to the altar, and linger in the aisles and corridors long after dismission to laugh and chat until one or two o'clock.

Then they go home to good dinners. Sometimes there is some special three o'clock service, but usually nothing save Sunday-school, until night. Then comes the chief meeting of the day; probably ten thousand Negroes gather every Sunday night in their churches. There is much music, much preaching, some short addresses; many strangers are there to be looked at; many beaus bring out their belles, and those who do not gather in crowds at the church door and escort the young women home. The crowds are usually well behaved and respectable, though rather more jolly than comports with a puritan idea of church services.

In this way the social life of the Negro centres in his church—baptism, wedding and burial, gossip and courtship, friendship and intrigue—all lie in these walls. What wonder that this central club house tends to become more and more luxuriously furnished, costly in appointment and easy of access!

It must not be inferred from all this that the Negro is hypocritical or irreligious. His church is, to be sure, a social institution first, and religious afterwards, but nevertheless, its religious activity is wide and sincere. In direct moral teaching and in setting moral standards for the people, however, the church is timid, and naturally so, for its constitution is democracy tempered by custom. Negro preachers are often condemned for poor leadership and empty sermons, and it is said that men with so much power and influence could make striking moral reforms. This is but partially true. The congregation does not follow the moral precepts of the preacher, but rather the preacher follows the standard of his flock, and only exceptional men dare seek to change this. And here it must be remembered that the Negro preacher is primarily an executive officer, rather than a spiritual guide. If one goes into any great Negro church and hears the sermon and views the audience, one would say: either the sermon is far below the calibre of the audience, or the people are less sensible than they look; the former explanation is usually true. The preacher is sure to be a man of executive ability, a leader of men, a shrewd and affable president of a large and intricate corporation. In addition to this he may be, and usually is, a striking elocutionist; he may also be a man of integrity, learning, and deep spiritual earnestness; but these last three are sometimes all lacking, and the last two in many cases. Some signs of advance are here manifest: no minister of notoriously immoral life, or even of bad reputation, could hold a large church in Philadelphia without eventual revolt. Most of the present pastors are decent, respectable men; there are perhaps one or two exceptions to this, but the exceptions are doubtful, rather than notorious. On the whole then, the average Negro preacher in this city is a shrewd manager, a respectable man, a good talker, a pleasant companion, but neither learned nor spiritual, nor a reformer.

The moral standards are therefore set by the congregations, and vary from church to church in some degree. There has been a slow working toward a literal obeying of the puritan and ascetic standard of morals which Methodism imposed on the freedmen; but condition and temperament have modified these. The grosser forms of immorality, together with theatre-going and dancing, are specifically denounced; nevertheless, the precepts against specific amusements are often violated by church members. The cleft between denominations is still wide, especially between Methodists and Baptists. The sermons are usually kept within the safe ground of a mild Calvinism, with much insistence on Salvation, Grace, Fallen Humanity and the like.

The chief function of these churches in morals is to conserve old standards and create about them a public opinion which shall deter the offender. And in this the Negro churches are peculiarly successful, although naturally the standards conserved are not as high as they should be.

4 STOREFRONT CHURCHES AND CULTS

For many newcomers the city was a strange, impersonal, and hostile place. The large conventional churches failed to provide the security or spiritual solace that had been found in the small congregations of the South. Some Negroes sought relief in tiny "storefront" churches or in new cults. Unfortunately, as this selection indicates, many unscrupulous men were ready to take advantage of this situation for their own personal gain.

From Ira De A. Reid, "Let Us Prey!" Opportunity 4 (September, 1926): 274–78. Reprinted by permission of the National Urban League.

Incredible as it may seem there are within the radius of one hundred and fifty blocks of that section of Harlem occupied by the colored population more than one hundred and forty churches. At the time of the count there were exactly that number. Since then more have been instituted or have moved into the district. These churches have an estimated membership of more than forty thousand.

One hundred and twenty-six of these institutions have become a part of the community since 1911 at which time the colored population was much below the 175,000 people who now give Harlem its local color. In the year mentioned there were fourteen churches. At that time the colored population was centered around the West Fifties and in the area west of Pennsylvania Station. There were to be found a few of the churches that have recently moved to more spacious and attractive quarters in Harlem. In that district one may yet find a large number of religious institutions that are filling the needs of the population that remains. But Harlem has been and is a magnet. As the people have come so have their institutions. Especially the churches.

In this large collection of religious institutions one may find the church respected and the church reviled, the church militant and the church penitent, the church "modern" and the church "fundamental," the church esoteric and the church exoteric. One may also find a diversified assortment of denominations—Baptist, Methodist, Presbyterian as well as Moravian, Lutheran, Apostolic and African Orthodox. And here is the mother church of the African Methodist Episcopal Zion Church, and the National Headquarters of the Eureka Oasis Discipleship.

There is no doubt that there are churches in each denomination rendering valuable service to the community. Unselfish and broad-minded ministers have realized the social value of the church and are interpreting it to their parishioners. . . .

However, these churches have an arduous task. Not only are they called upon to minister to the social and religious needs of their people, but they must also keep established a defense mechanism to offset the subtle encroachments of a large number of smaller institutions called churches, whose leaders have advertently or inadvertently revised the well-known entreaty to prayer. For them it reads "Let us prey."

Only fifty-four of these churches are housed in regular church edifices, or residences that have been converted to a peculiar style of church architecture. The churches remaining are in the class known as house churches. They are to be found occupying the first floor of a private dwelling, a site formerly used for business purposes, or the back room of a flat. In fact they are anywhere and everywhere. Yet one cannot register a wholesale criticism against a church because it is located in a house, for there are many larger churches whose general conduct is less moral. It is likewise true that many of the larger churches have had their beginning in houses. Nor can one evade the fact that in this same group there is found a large number of so-called churches that do little or no good and much harm in the community. . . .

Ministers of the leading churches in this section have been opposed to this spurious growth of so-called Christian churches for some time, and have violently condemned the esoteric cults that have arisen. The latter are in most cases conducted by exploiters and charlatans. But they are dynamically opposed to the activities of the "one-man" church. The pastor of one of the largest churches said in a sermon a few weeks ago: "No we haven't too many churches in Harlem. We do have too many house churches. Somebody wants to be a leader, deacon or preacher and if the large church doesn't give it to him he will establish a little church of his own where he can be seen. Selfishness is really the cause of so many of these house churches." Thus speaks one. And many others have been more violent. Yet these churches have increased.

The churches that spasmodically arise from nowhere and in many cases disappear in much the same fashion are a general nuisance. Neither their appearance nor their character warrants the respect of the community. Their ministers are familiarly called "jack-legs," while their poorly written sign-boards advertising the name of the pastor with his title and degrees, and incidentally the name of the church and the order of service have become the butt of many jokes. Look at one. This holy tabernacle of God is in the very heart of Harlem. One thinks of all save church as he sees a dilapidated frame structure panting beneath the crush of two brick buildings that have been erected on either side of it. There is a yard. A hungry cat slinks through the gate. She reposes on an old push cart in the yard. One sees a rusty milk can, a cot, and several well-aged pieces of wood scattered promiscuously in front of the entrance. An old stone walk leads to the door. It is well worn and cracked. The crevices have been worn to the level of the walk. The steps have been patched so often that little of the original framework seems to remain. The house is paintless except in isolated spots. A dry-rotted trellis hangs dejectedly down the side. In the basement a carpenter plies his trade awaiting the coming of such persons as will follow his teachings blatantly expressed on the shingle which reads:

> *We Believe That All Manner of Disease Can Be Cured*
> by the power of GOD divine. Healing is always needed; no matter what your ailment may be it can always be cured. This place is open day and night for the healing of the sick and prayer.
>> *Jesus is the Doctor*
>> *Services on Sunday*

In this group of churches there were fifty meeting in places that had outlived their usefulness as homes or places of business. These places rarely if ever seat fifty persons at the utmost, and are poorly lighted and ventilated. They are chiefly immediate neighborhood affairs, support depending upon the activity of the pastor in securing members from the surrounding apartments and tenements. It is because of this fact that the turnover among these churches is very high. They are forced to follow their members, secure new ones, or go out of business. Six weeks after the preliminary list of the churches was made seven of the churches previously listed could not be found.

The wrath of the public when it is active is centered upon the ministers of these churches rather than at the churches themselves. It is the feeling that they are the ones responsible for such a condition. But they must live and despite what may be said against them it is true that in them you find one group that is doing the thing it wants to do. There is no doubt that the assertion made by a minister that selfishness was the underlying motive of many of the organizations is true. One is reminded of the incident relating to the young swain who had come to the church meeting to show good reason why he should be ordained as a Christian minister. He stated that he had a dream. In this dream a still small voice told him to "G. P. C." and when he heard it he knew that he was instructed to "Go preach Christ." After further questioning by the council the chairman told him that he had misinterpreted his dream, for it certainly meant "Go plant corn." . . .

All these things do not loom as large upon the horizon of church problems as does the rapid growth of the church esoteric in Harlem. Within the last six years there has been a tidal wave of these groups, many of them sincere in their beliefs but hampered and degraded by a large number of exploiters and charlatans. There are they who dabble in spiritualism, exhibiting their many charms and wares in the form of Grand Imperial incense, prayer incense, aluminum trumpets, luminous bands and other accessories. Among the exploiters in this group one is wont to find as many women as men engaged as pastors, directors and leaders.

It is astounding to note the growth and variety of these movements. Here one finds "The Commandment Keepers, Holy Church of the Living God, The Pillar and the Ground of the Truth," "The Temple of the Gospel of the Kingdom," "The Metaphysical Church of the Divine Investigation," "Prophet Bess," "Mt. Zion Pentecostal Church," "St. Matthew's Church of the Divine Silence and Truth," "Tabernacle of the Congregation of the Disciples of the Kingdom," "Congregation of Beth B'Nai Abraham," "Holy Temple of God in Christ," "The Church of the Temple of Love," and many others—all practicing various doctrines and creeds provocative of no good save the financial returns obtained by the leader.

A visit to the average fake spiritualist meeting proves to be of an innocent if not stupid nature. There are possibly ten or twelve believers present when the service begins. Terrible discords and hymns that were deserving of a better fate were sung. Then the plate was passed and the leader or the assistant passed the plate, appealing for funds to pay the rent already past due. Then the messages started.

This medium, who chanced to be an immense fat man, used none of the regular tricks of the trade. He relied upon the stupidity of the audience and his own. After a few convulsive shivers he started to get messages.

Standing in front of each person in turn, and holding some article belonging to him, he proceeded to bring him the good word from those who had passed beyond. Half of the time the messages were wrong, most of the time they were so general they could be applied to any one, and the rest of the time they were so jumbled nobody could understand them. The whole thing was a farce yet one old man sat in the meeting, paid the medium his two dollars—that he evidently needed very badly for himself —and listened with tears in his eyes to the message from a dead relative. The medium failed to mention just which relative it was.

This medium belonged to the "piker" class. There are some who charge larger fees and work with all the paraphernalia of the profession. They get their messages in the dark and have various ways of speaking through collapsible trumpets, and tapping those who are to receive the messages. They prey upon people whose better judgment has been deadened by worry or sorrow, and reap an immense profit. Most of the people thus engaged are in the business for easy personal gain, and are out and out frauds, although there are some sincere mediums and some sincere spiritualists.

This prostitution does not stop here. There have infested Harlem groups that to all appearances have "acquired" the distinguishing features of the Jews and have called themselves Black Jews. They claim to have come from Damascus, Palestine, and various parts of the Orient. Their activities range from a grocery store to a conservatory of music.

Recently the head of one of these cults has been sent to the Federal Penitentiary for the violation of the Mann Act. This group conducted a "baby farm" in Abescon, N.J. Here was said to be the home of the many children of the "Messiah" (who was their leader). They were borne by such "virgins" as had been elected by him to give themselves to the propagation of the cause. Here are Elder Lazarus, Elder Kauffman, Rosenthal, Goldberg, and many other interesting characters. Under their leadership the Temple of the Gospel of the Kingdom continues. . . .

Then there are other cults that function in their own peculiar fashion. A former minister of the Methodist church, who resigned in 1913, conducts a clannish thing called a Discipleship. There are associated and initiated members. When this minister became the founder and head of the sect he assumed the title of Bishop and the degree of D.D.T.

In this group when one has earned the title of Disciple there is erected in his or her home an altar. The Disciple is now qualified to minister to the physical and spiritual wants of those who are willing to believe. Their services are conducted under such high-sounding phrases as "The Sanctiloquent Equity Exposition," "Inquisition and Information Service," "Practical Biblical Deliberation," and "Ethical Development Classes."

The whole group is characterized by the machinations of impostors who do their work in great style. Bishops without a diocese, those who heal with divine inspiration, praying circles that charge for their services, American Negroes turned Jews "over night," theological seminaries conducted in the rear of "railroad" apartments, Black Rev. Wm. Sundays, Ph.D., who have escaped the wrath of many communities, new denominations built upon the fundamental doctrine of race—all these and even more contribute to the prostitution of the church. And there seems to be no end to their growth. Already have five new institutions been opened for business. One thinks of the much advertised cinema production "Hell Bent For Heaven."

Despite the great religious cooperative efforts that have been launched in Harlem and are associated with similar groups throughout the city one cannot overlook the grim picture that exists. While the organized churches have been the source of much good the others have been a troublesome briar. Where one has progressed in the type of ministers selected and in the reformation of the church program, the other has become stuffed with cast-offs and religious criminals who will not be denied. While the aggressive minority is pushing forward with intelligent and modern interpretation of a gospel that was once wholly emotionalized, the satellites have glittered with their emotional paroxysms and illusive and illiterate mysticisms.

It is unfortunate that the efforts of sincere and well-established churches in Harlem, both small and large, have to be hampered by the manipulations of these groups—both orthodox and pagan—of the outer fringe. While the one steadily prods at social problems with instruments both spiritual and physical, and methods religious and humanitarian, the others are saying "Let us prey." And they do.

5   URBANIZATION AND THE NEGRO FAMILY

If the authority of the traditional churches was weakened in the city, so were the family ties that had been nourished in a rural environment strained by the forces of urban life. In this selection, written in the 1930s, the influential Negro sociologist, E. Franklin Frazier, warns about the adverse effects of the city on the Negro family.

From E. Franklin Frazier, The Negro Family in the United States *(Chicago: The University of Chicago Press, 1939), pp. 484–88. Copyright 1939 by the University of Chicago Press. Reprinted by permission of the publisher.*

. . . [T]he urbanization of the Negro population since 1900 has brought the most momentous change in the family life of the Negro since emancipation. This movement, which has carried a million Negroes to southern cities alone, has torn the Negro loose from his cultural moorings. Thousands of these migrants have been solitary men and women who have led a more or less lawless sex life during their wanderings. But many more illiterate or semi-illiterate and impoverished Negro families, broken or held together only by the fragile bonds of sympathy and habit, have sought a dwelling-place in the slums of southern cities. Because of the dissolution of the rural folkways and mores, the children in these families have helped to swell the ranks of juvenile delinquents. Likewise, the bonds of sympathy and community of interests that held their parents together in the rural environment have been unable to withstand the disintegrating forces in the city. Illegitimacy, which was a more or less harmless affair in the country, has become a serious economic and social problem. At times students of social problems have seen in these various aspects of family disorganization a portent of the Negro's destruction

During and following the World War, the urbanization of the Negro population was accelerated and acquired even greater significance than earlier migrations to cities. The Negro was carried beyond the small southern cities and plunged into the midst of modern industrial centers in the North. Except for the war period, when there was a great demand for his labor, the migration of the Negro to northern cities has forced him into a much more rigorous type of competition with whites than he has ever faced. Because of his rural background and ignorance, he has entered modern industry as a part of the great army of unskilled workers. Like the immigrant groups that have preceded him, he has been forced to live in the slum areas of northern cities. In vain social workers and others have constantly held conferences on the housing conditions of Negroes, but they have been forced finally to face the fundamental fact of the Negro's poverty. Likewise, social and welfare agencies have been unable to stem the tide of family disorganization that has followed as a natural consequence of the impact of modern civilization upon the folkways and mores of a simple peasant folk. Even Negro families with traditions of stable family life have not been unaffected by the social and economic forces in urban communities. Family traditions and social distinctions that had meaning and significance in the relatively simple and stable southern communities have lost their meaning in the new world of the modern city

One of the most important consequences of the urbanization of the Negro has been the rapid occupational differentiation of the population. A Negro middle class has come into existence as the result of new opportunities and greater freedom as well as the new demands of the awakened Negro communities for all kinds of services. This change in the structure of Negro life has been rapid and has not had time to solidify. The old

stablished families, generally of mulatto origin, have looked with con-
empt upon the new middle class which has come into prominence as the
esult of successful competition in the new environment. With some truth
n their side, they have complained that these newcomers lack the culture,
tability in family life, and purity of morals which characterized their
own class when it graced the social pyramid. In fact, there has not been
ufficient time for these new strata to form definite patterns of family life.
Consequently, there is much confusion and conflict in ideals and aims
nd patterns of behavior which have been taken over as the result of the
arious types of suggestion and imitation in the urban environment.

The most significant element in the new social structure of Negro life
s the black industrial proletariat that has been emerging since the Negro
vas introduced into Western civilization. Its position in industry in the
North was insecure and of small consequence until, with the cessation of
oreign immigration during the World War, it became a permanent part
of the industrial proletariat. This development has affected tremendously
he whole outlook on life and the values of the masses of Negroes. Here-
ofore, the Negro was chiefly a worker in domestic and personal services,
nd his ideals of family and other aspects of life were a crude imitation of
he middle-class standards which he saw. Very often in the hotel or club
e saw the white man during his leisure and recreation and therefore
cquired leisure-class ideals which have probably been responsible for the
'sporting complex" and the thriftlessness which are widespread among
Negroes. But thousands of Negroes are becoming accustomed to the
discipline of modern industry and are developing habits of consumption
onsonant with their new role. As the Negro has become an industrial
vorker and received adequate compensation, the father has become the
chief breadwinner and assumed a responsible place in his family.

When one views in retrospect the waste of human life, the immorality,
delinquency, desertions, and broken homes which have been involved in
he development of Negro family life in the United States, they appear to
have been the inevitable consequences of the attempt of a preliterate
people, stripped of their cultural heritage, to adjust themselves to civiliza-
ion. The very fact that the Negro has succeeded in adopting habits of
living that have enabled him to survive in a civilization based upon laissez
aire and competition, itself bespeaks a degree of success in taking on the
olkways and mores of the master race. That the Negro has found within
he patterns of the white man's culture a purpose in life and a significance
or his strivings which have involved sacrifices for his children and the
urbing of individual desires and impulses indicates that he has become
ssimilated to a new mode of life.

However, when one undertakes to envisage the probable course of
development of the Negro family in the future, it appears that the travail
of civilization is not yet ended. First it appears that the family which

evolved within the isolated world of the Negro folk will become increas ingly disorganized. Modern means of communication will break down the isolation of the world of black folk, and, as long as the bankrupt system of southern agriculture exists, Negro families will continue to seek a living in the towns and cities of the country. They will crowd the slum areas of southern cities or make their way to northern cities where their family life will become disrupted and their poverty will force them to depend upon charity. Those families that possess some heritage of family tradition and education will resist the destructive forces of urban life more success fully than the illiterate Negro folk. In either case their family life will adapt itself to the secular and rational organization of urban life. Un doubtedly, there will be a limitation of offspring; and men and women who associate in marriage will use it as a means for individual develop ment.

The process of assimilation and acculturation in a highly mobile and urbanized society will proceed on a different basis from that in the past. There are evidences at present that in the urban environment, where caste prescriptions lose their force, Negroes and whites in the same occupational classes are being drawn into closer association than in the past. Such associations, to be sure, are facilitating the assimilation of only the more formal aspects of white civilization; but there are signs that intermarriage in the future will bring about a fundamental type of assimilation. But, in the final analysis, the process of assimilation and acculturation will be limited by the extent to which the Negro becomes integrated into the economic organization and participates in the life of the community. The gains in civilization which result from participation in the white world will in the future as in the past be transmitted to future generations through the family.

6   THE MOYNIHAN REPORT

According to a report prepared in March, 1965, by then Assistant Secretary of Labor Daniel P. Moynihan, the disorganization of the Negro family which E. Franklin Frazier had prophesied had come about to an alarming degree. The report became an immediate subject of intense controversy. Critics felt that Moynihan greatly overstated the differences between white and black families and that, regardless of his intent, the report provided ammunition for anti-Negro racists. At any rate, the report did indicate a recognition of the fact that with the great shift of Negroes from the rural South to the city, civil rights advocates had to become more concerned with the socioeconomic, as opposed to purely legal, obstacles to full equality.

From Daniel P. Moynihan, The Negro Family: The Case for National Action (*Washington, D.C.: Government Printing Office, 1965), pp. 5–6, 8–14, 47–48.*

At the heart of the deterioration of the fabric of Negro society is the deterioration of the Negro family.

It is the fundamental source of the weakness of the Negro community at the present time.

There is probably no single fact of Negro American life so little understood by whites. The Negro situation is commonly perceived by whites in terms of the visible manifestations of discrimination and poverty, in part because Negro protest is directed against such obstacles, and in part, no doubt, because these are facts which involve the actions and attitudes of the white community as well. It is more difficult, however, for whites to perceive the effect that three centuries of exploitation have had on the fabric of Negro society itself. Here the consequences of the historic injustices done to Negro Americans are silent and hidden from view. But here is where the true injury has occurred: unless this damage is repaired, all the effort to end discrimination and poverty and injustice will come to little.

The role of the family in shaping character and ability is so pervasive as to be easily overlooked. The family is the basic social unit of American life; it is the basic socializing unit. By and large, adult conduct in society is learned as a child.

A fundamental insight of psychoanalytic theory, for example, is that the child learns a way of looking at life in his early years through which all later experience is viewed and which profoundly shapes his adult conduct.

It may be hazarded that the reason family structure does not loom larger in public discussion of social issues is that people tend to assume that the nature of family life is about the same throughout American society. The mass media and the development of suburbia have created an image of the American family as a highly standardized phenomenon. It is therefore easy to assume that whatever it is that makes for differences among individuals or groups of individuals, it is not a different family structure.

There is much truth to this; as with any other nation, Americans ar producing a recognizable family system. But that process is not complete by any means. There are still, for example, important differences i family patterns surviving from the age of the great European migratio to the United States, and these variations account for notable difference in the progress and assimilation of various ethnic and religious group. A number of immigrant groups were characterized by unusually stron family bonds; these groups have characteristically progressed more rap idly than others.

But there is one truly great discontinuity in family structure in th United States at the present time: that between the white world i general and that of the Negro American.

The white family has achieved a high degree of stability and is main taining that stability.

By contrast, the family structure of lower-class Negroes is highly unstable, an in many urban centers is approaching complete breakdown.

N.b. There is considerable evidence that the Negro community is i fact dividing between a stable middle-class group that is steadily growin stronger and more successful, and an increasingly disorganized and dis advantaged lower-class group. There are indications, for example, tha the middle-class Negro family puts a higher premium on family stabilit and the conserving of family resources than does the white middle-clas family. The discussion of this paper is not, obviously, directed to the firs group excepting as it is affected by the experiences of the second—a important exception. . . .

There are two points to be noted in this context.

First, the emergence and increasing visibility of a Negro middle clas may beguile the nation into supposing that the circumstances of th remainder of the Negro community are equally prosperous, whereas jus the opposite is true at present, and is likely to continue so.

Second, the lumping of all Negroes together in one statistical measure ment very probably conceals the extent of the disorganization amon the lower-class group. If conditions are improving for one and deterio rating for the other, the resultant statistical averages might show n change. Further, the statistics on the Negro family and most other sub jects treated in this paper refer only to a specific point in time. They ar a vertical measure of the situation at a given moment. They do no measure the experience of individuals over time. Thus the averag monthly unemployment rate for Negro males for 1964 is recorded a 9 per cent. But *during* 1964, some 29 per cent of Negro males were un employed at one time or another. Similarly, for example, if 36 per cen of Negro children are living in broken homes *at any specific moment*, it i likely that a far higher proportion of Negro children find themselves i that situation *at one time or another* in their lives.

NEARLY A QUARTER OF URBAN NEGRO MARRIAGES ARE DISSOLVED

Nearly a quarter of Negro women living in cities who have ever married are divorced, separated, or are living apart from their husbands.

The rates are highest in the urban Northeast where 26 per cent of Negro women ever married are either divorced, separated, or have their husbands absent.

On the urban frontier, the proportion of husbands absent is even higher. In New York City in 1960, it was 30.2 per cent, *not* including divorces.

Among ever-married nonwhite women in the nation, the proportion with husbands present *declined* in *every* age group over the decade 1950–60, as follows:

Age	Per Cent with Husbands Present	
	1950	*1960*
15–19 years	77.8	72.5
20–24 years	76.7	74.2
25–29 years	76.1	73.4
30–34 years	74.9	72.0
35–39 years	73.1	70.7
40–44 years	68.9	68.2

Although similar declines occurred among white females, the proportion of white husbands present never dropped below 90 per cent except for the first and last age group.

NEARLY ONE-QUARTER OF NEGRO BIRTHS ARE NOW ILLEGITIMATE

Both white and Negro illegitimacy rates have been increasing, although from dramatically different bases. The white rate was 2 per cent in 1940; it was 3.07 per cent in 1963. In that period, the Negro rate went from 16.8 per cent to 23.6 per cent.

The number of illegitimate children per 1,000 live births increased by 11 among whites in the period 1940–63, but by 68 among nonwhites. There are, of course, limits to the dependability of these statistics. There are almost certainly a considerable number of Negro children who, although technically illegitimate, are in fact the offspring of stable unions. On the other hand, it may be assumed that many births that are in fact illegitimate are recorded otherwise. Probably the two opposite effects cancel each other out.

On the urban frontier, the nonwhite illegitimacy rates are usually higher than the national average, and the increase of late has been drastic.

In the District of Columbia, the illegitimacy rate for nonwhites grew from 21.8 per cent in 1950, to 29.5 per cent in 1964.

A similar picture of disintegrating Negro marriages emerges from the divorce statistics. Divorces have increased of late for both whites and nonwhites, but at a much greater rate for the latter. In 1940 both groups had a divorce rate of 2.2 per cent. By 1964 the white rate had risen to 3.6 per cent, but the nonwhite rate had reached 5.1 per cent—40 per cent greater than the formerly equal white rate.

ALMOST ONE-FOURTH OF NEGRO FAMILIES ARE HEADED BY FEMALES

As a direct result of this high rate of divorce, separation, and desertion, a very large per cent of Negro families are headed by females. While the percentage of such families among whites has been dropping since 1940, it has been rising among Negroes.

The per cent of nonwhite families headed by a female is more than double the per cent for whites. Fatherless nonwhite families increased by a sixth between 1950 and 1960, but held constant for white families.

It has been estimated that only a minority of Negro children reach the age of 18 having lived all their lives with both their parents.

Once again, this measure of family disorganization is found to be diminishing among white families and increasing among Negro families.

THE BREAKDOWN OF THE NEGRO FAMILY HAS LED TO A STARTLING INCREASE IN WELFARE DEPENDENCY

The majority of Negro children receive public assistance under the AFDC program at one point or another in their childhood.

At present, 14 per cent of Negro children are receiving AFDC assistance, as against 2 per cent of white children. Eight per cent of white children receive such assistance at some time, as against 56 per cent of nonwhites, according to an extrapolation based on HEW data. (Let it be noted, however, that out of a total of 1.8 million nonwhite illegitimate children in the nation in 1961, 1.3 million were *not* receiving aid under the AFDC program, although a substantial number have, or will, receive aid at some time in their lives.)

Again, the situation may be said to be worsening. The AFDC program, deriving from the long established Mothers' Aid programs, was established in 1935 principally to care for widows and orphans, although the legislation covered all children in homes deprived of parental support because one or both of their parents are absent or incapacitated.

In the beginning, the number of AFDC families in which the father was absent because of desertion was less than a third of the total. Today it is two-thirds. HEW estimates "that between two-thirds and three-fourths of the 50 per cent increase from 1948 to 1955 in the number of absent-father families receiving ADC may be explained by an increase in broken homes in the population."

A 1960 study of Aid to Dependent Children in Cook County, Ill. stated:

> The "typical" ADC mother in Cook County was married and had children by her husband, who deserted; his whereabouts are unknown, and he does not contribute to the support of his children. She is not free to remarry and has had an illegitimate child since her husband left. (Almost 90 percent of the ADC families are Negro.)

The steady expansion of this welfare program, as of public assistance programs in general, can be taken as a measure of the steady disintegration of the Negro family structure over the past generation in the United States.

• • •

The object of this study has been to define a problem, rather than propose solutions to it. We have kept within these confines for three reasons.

First, there are many persons, within and without the Government, who do not feel the problem exists, at least in any serious degree. These persons feel that, with the legal obstacles to assimilation out of the way, matters will take care of themselves in the normal course of events. This is a fundamental issue, and requires a decision within the Government.

Second, it is our view that the problem is so interrelated, one thing with another, that any list of program proposals would necessarily be incomplete, and would distract attention from the main point of interrelatedness. We have shown a clear relation between male employment, for example, and the number of welfare dependent children. Employment in turn reflects educational achievement, which depends in large part on family stability, which reflects employment. Where we should break into this cycle, and how, are the most difficult domestic questions facing the United States. We must first reach agreement on what the problem is, then we will know what questions must be answered.

Third, it is necessary to acknowledge the view, held by a number of responsible persons, that this problem may in fact be out of control. This is a view with which we emphatically and totally disagree, but the view must be acknowledged. The persistent rise in Negro educational achievement is probably the main trend that belies this thesis. On the other hand our study has produced some clear indications that the situation may indeed have begun to feed on itself. It may be noted, for example, that for most of the post-war period male Negro unemployment and the number of new AFDC cases rose and fell together as if connected by a chain from 1948 to 1962. The correlation between the two series of data was an astonishing .91. (This would mean that 83 per cent of the rise and fall in AFDC cases can be statistically ascribed to the rise and fall in the unemployment rate.) In 1960, however, for the first time, unemployment declined, but the number of new AFDC cases rose. In 1963 this happened a second time. In 1964 a third. The possible implications of these and other data are serious enough that they, too, should be understood before program proposals are made.

However, the argument of this paper does lead to one central conclusion: Whatever the specific elements of a national effort designed to resolve this problem, those elements must be coordinated in terms of one general strategy.

What then is that problem? We feel the answer is clear enough. Three centuries of injustice have brought about deep-seated structural distortions in the life of the Negro American. At this point, the present tangle of pathology is capable of perpetuating itself without assistance from the white world. The cycle can be broken only if these distortions are set right.

In a word, a national effort towards the problems of Negro Americans must be directed towards the question of family structure. The object should be to strengthen the Negro family so as to enable it to raise and support its members as do other families. After that, how this group of Americans chooses to run its affairs, take advantage of its opportunities, or fail to do so, is none of the nation's business.

The fundamental importance and urgency of restoring the Negro American family structure has been evident for some time. E. Franklin Frazier put it most succinctly in 1950:

> As the result of family disorganization a large proportion of Negro children and youth have not undergone the socialization which only the family can provide. The disorganized families have failed to provide for their emotional needs and have not provided the discipline and habits which are necessary for personality development. Because the disorganized family has failed in its function as a socializing agency, it has handicapped the children in their relations to the institutions in the community. Moreover, family disorganization has been partially responsible for a large amount of juvenile delinquency and adult crime among Negroes. Since the widespread family disorganization among Negroes has resulted from the failure of the father to play the role in family life required by American society, the mitigation of this problem must await those changes in the Negro and American society which will enable the Negro father to play the role required of him.

Nothing was done in response to Frazier's argument. Matters were left to take care of themselves, and as matters will, grew worse, not better.

The problem is now more serious, the obstacles greater. There is, however, a profound change for the better in one respect. The President has committed the nation to an all-out effort to eliminate poverty wherever it exists, among whites or Negroes, and a militant, organized, and responsible Negro movement exists to join in that effort. Such a national effort could be stated thus:

The policy of the United States is to bring the Negro American to full and equal sharing in the responsibilities and rewards of citizenship. To this end, the programs of the Federal government bearing on this objective shall be designed to have the effect, directly or indirectly, of enhancing the stability and resources of the Negro American family.

VI Urban Violence

The violent eruptions that have broken out in so many black ghettos since 1964 have led to dire predictions about the future of American cities. Terrible though these disorders have been, it is instructive to recognize that mob action and violence have marred the urban scene in America since at least the beginning of the eighteenth century. The particular causes of the early riots have varied, with labor or religious conflict and opposition to the Civil War draft accounting for some of the worst in the nineteenth century. Urban race riots date from the beginning of the twentieth century. One student has counted thirty-three major outbreaks from 1900 to 1949, with twenty-two of them occurring between 1915 and 1919.* The disorders of the 1960s have differed from the earlier ones in the extent to which Negroes have themselves assumed the initiative, especially in the extensive destruction of property. In all cases the major victims have been black, and police brutality has been an old and persistent theme. Moreover, a comparison of the recommendations made by the Chicago Commission on Race Relations in 1922, some of which are reprinted below, with more recent reports on urban violence makes clear to a depressing degree the extent to which the cities have failed to change the conditions that have contributed so greatly to the interracial tension.

* Richard Maxwell Brown, "Historical Patterns of Violence in America." In Hugh Davis Graham and Ted Robert Gurr, eds., *Violence in America: Historical and Comparative Perspectives*, A Report Submitted to the National Commission on the Causes and Prevention of Violence (New York: Bantam Books, 1969), pp. 53–55.

ATLANTA 1906: WALTER WHITE ▸ISCOVERS HIS IDENTITY

native of Atlanta, Georgia, Walter White was first appointed to the
ff of the NAACP in 1918 and later served for many years as its
ecutive Secretary. Much of his early work with the NAACP was
voted to the investigation of lynchings. His personal knowledge of
olence began as a boy when he witnessed the anti-Negro outbreak in
tlanta in September of 1906. Although he was light-skinned and was
ten mistaken for white, the night of terror in Atlanta confirmed his
wavering identity as a Negro.

om Walter White, A Man Called White (*New York: The*
king Press, Inc., 1948), pp. 4–12. Copyright 1948 by Walter
hite. Reprinted by permission of The Viking Press, Inc.

There is no mistake. I am a Negro. There can be no doubt. I know
e night when, in terror and bitterness of soul, I discovered that I was
t apart by the pigmentation of my skin (invisible though it was in my
se) and the moment at which I decided that I would infinitely rather
what I was than, through taking advantage of the way of escape that
as open to me, be one of the race which had forced the decision upon me.

There were nine light-skinned Negroes in my family: mother, father,
ve sisters, an older brother, George, and myself. The house in which I
scovered what it meant to be a Negro was located on Houston Street,
ree blocks from the Candler Building, Atlanta's first skyscraper, which
re the name of the ex-drug clerk who had become a millionaire from
e sale of Coca-Cola. Below us lived none but Negroes; toward town all
t a very few were white. Ours was an eight-room, two-story frame house
hich stood out in its surroundings not because of its opulence but by
ntrast with the drabness and unpaintedness of the other dwellings in a
teriorating neighborhood.

Only Father kept his house painted, the picket fence repaired, the
ard fence separating our place from those on either side whitewashed,
e grass neatly trimmed, and flower beds abloom. Mother's passion for
atness was even more pronounced and it seemed to me that I was
ways the victim of her determination to see no single blade of grass

longer than the others or any one of the pickets in the front fence le
shiny with paint than its mates. This spic-and-spanness became increa
ingly apparent as the rest of the neighborhood became more down-at-hee
and resulted, as we were to learn, in sullen envy among some of our whi
neighbors. It was the violent expression of that resentment against a Negr
family neater than themselves which set the pattern of our lives.

On a day in September 1906, when I was thirteen, we were taught tha
there is no isolation from life. The unseasonably oppressive heat of a
Indian summer day hung like a steaming blanket over Atlanta. My siste
and I had casually commented upon the unusual quietness. It seemed t
stay Mother's volubility and reduced Father, who was more taciturn, t
monosyllables. But, as I remember it, no other sense of impending troub
impinged upon our consciousness.

I had read the inflammatory headlines in the *Atlanta News* and th
more restrained ones in the *Atlanta Constitution* which reported allege
rapes and other crimes committed by Negroes. But these were so standar
and familiar that they made—as I look back on it now—little impressio
The stories were more frequent, however, and consisted of eight-colum
streamers instead of the usual two- or four-column ones.

Father was a mail collector. His tour of duty was from three to eleve
P.M. He made his rounds in a little cart into which one climbed from
step in the rear. I used to drive the cart for him from two until seve
leaving him at the point nearest our home on Houston Street, to retur
home either for study or sleep. That day Father decided that I should n
go with him. I appealed to Mother, who thought it might be all righ
provided Father sent me home before dark because, she said, "I don
think they would dare start anything before nightfall." Father told me ;
we made the rounds that ominous rumors of a race riot that night we;
sweeping the town. But I was too young that morning to understand th
background of the riot. I became much older during the next thirty-s
hours, under circumstances which I now recognize as the inevitable ou
come of what had preceded.

One of the most bitter political campaigns of that bloody era w
reaching its climax. Hoke Smith—that amazing contradiction of co
rageous and intelligent opposition to the South's economic ills and at th
same time advocacy of ruthless suppression of the Negro—was a candida
that year for the governorship. His opponent was Clark Howell, editor
the *Atlanta Constitution*, which boasted with justification that it "cove
Dixie like the dew." Howell and his supporters held firm authority ov
the state Democratic machine despite the long and bitter fight Hoke Smi
had made on Howell in the columns of the rival *Atlanta Journal*. . .

To overcome the power of the regular Democratic organization, Ho
Smith sought to heal the feud of long standing between himself and th
powerful ex-radical Populist, Thomas E. Watson. . . .

The two rabble-rousers stumped the state screaming, "Nigger, nigger, nigger!" Some white farmers still believed Watson's abandoned doctrine that the interests of Negro and white farmers and industrial workers were identical. They feared that Watson's and Smith's new scheme to disfranchise Negro voters would lead to disfranchisement of poor whites. Tom Watson was sent to trade on his past reputation to reassure them that such was not the case and that their own interests were best served by now hating "niggers." . . .

At the same time, a daily newspaper was attempting to wrest from the *Atlanta Journal* leadership in the afternoon field. The new paper, the *Atlanta News*, in its scramble for circulation and advertising took a lesson from the political race and began to play up in eight-column streamers stories of the raping of white women by Negroes. That every one of the stories was afterward found to be wholly without foundation was of no importance. The *News* circulation, particularly in street sales, leaped swiftly upward as the headlines were bawled by lusty-voiced newsboys. Atlanta became a tinder box. . . .

During the afternoon preceding the riot little bands of sullen, evil-looking men talked excitedly on street corners all over downtown Atlanta. Around seven o'clock my father and I were driving toward a mail box at the corner of Peachtree and Houston Streets when there came from near-by Pryor Street a roar the like of which I had never heard before, but which sent a sensation of mingled fear and excitement coursing through my body. I asked permission of Father to go and see what the trouble was. He bluntly ordered me to stay in the cart. A little later we drove down Atlanta's main business thoroughfare, Peachtree Street. Again we heard the terrifying cries, this time near at hand and coming toward us. We saw a lame Negro bootblack from Herndon's barber shop pathetically trying to outrun a mob of whites. Less than a hundred yards from us the chase ended. We saw clubs and fists descending to the accompaniment of savage shouting and cursing. Suddenly a voice cried, "There goes another nigger!" Its work done, the mob went after new prey. The body with the withered foot lay dead in a pool of blood on the street.

Father's apprehension and mine steadily increased during the evening, although the fact that our skins were white kept us from attack. Another circumstance favored us—the mob had not yet grown violent enough to attack United States government property. But I could see Father's relief when he punched the time clock at eleven P.M. and got into the cart to go home. He wanted to go the back way down Forsyth Street, but I begged him, in my childish excitement and ignorance, to drive down Marietta to Five Points, the heart of Atlanta's business district, where the crowds were densest and the yells loudest. No sooner had we turned into Marietta Street, however, than we saw careening toward us an undertaker's barouche. Crouched in the rear of the vehicle were three Negroes clinging to the sides of the carriage as it lunged and swerved. On the driver's seat crouched a white man, the reins held taut in his left hand. A huge whip was gripped in his right. Alternately he lashed the horses and, without looking backward, swung the whip in savage swoops in the faces o members of the mob as they lunged at the carriage, determined to seize the three Negroes.

There was no time for us to get out of its path, so sudden and swift was the appearance of the vehicle. The hub cap of the right rear wheel of the barouche hit the right side of our much lighter wagon. Father and I instinctively threw our weight and kept the cart from turning completely over. Our mare was a Texas mustang which, frightened by the sudden blow, lunged in the air as Father clung to the reins. Good fortune was with us. The cart settled back on its four wheels as Father said in a voice which brooked no dissent, "We are going home the back way and not down Marietta."

But again on Pryor Street we heard the cry of the mob. Close to us and in our direction ran a stout and elderly woman who cooked at a downtown white hotel. Fifty yards behind, a mob which filled the street from curb to curb was closing in. Father handed the reins to me and, though he was of slight stature, reached down and lifted the woman into the cart. I did not need to be told to lash the mare to the fastest speed she could muster.

The church bells tolled the next morning for Sunday service. But no one in Atlanta believed for a moment that the hatred and lust for blood had been appeased. Like skulls on a cannibal's hut the hats and caps of victims of the mob of the night before had been hung on the iron hooks of telegraph poles. None could tell whether each hat represented a dead Negro. But we knew that some of those who had worn the hats would never again wear any.

Late in the afternoon friends of my father's came to warn of more trouble that night. They told us that plans had been perfected for a mob to form on Peachtree Street just after nightfall to march down Houston Street to what the white people called "Darktown," three blocks or so below our house, to "clean out the niggers." There had never been a firearm in our house before that day. Father was reluctant even in those circumstances to violate the law, but he at last gave in at Mother's insistence.

We turned out the lights early, as did all our neighbors. No one removed his clothes or thought of sleep. Apprehension was tangible. We could almost touch its cold and clammy surface. Toward midnight the unnatural quiet was broken by a roar that grew steadily in volume. Even today I grow tense in remembering it.

Father told Mother to take my sisters, the youngest of them only six, to the rear of the house, which offered more protection from stones and bullets. My brother George was away, so Father and I, the only males in the house, took our places at the front windows of the parlor. The windows opened on a porch along the front side of the house, which in turn gave onto a narrow lawn that sloped down to the street and a picket fence. There was a crash as Negroes smashed the street lamp at the corner of Houston and Piedmont Avenue down the street. In a very few minutes the vanguard of the mob, some of them bearing torches, appeared. A voice which we recognized as that of the son of the grocer with whom we had traded for many years yelled, "That's where that nigger mail carrier lives! Let's burn it down! It's too nice for a nigger to live in!" In the eerie light Father turned his drawn face toward me. In a voice as quiet as though he were asking me to pass him the sugar at the breakfast table, he said, "Son, don't shoot until the first man puts his foot on the lawn and then—don't you miss!"

In the flickering light the mob swayed, paused, and began to flow toward us. In that instant there opened up within me a great awareness; I knew then who I was. I was a Negro, a human being with an invisible pigmentation which marked me a person to be hunted, hanged, abused, discriminated against, kept in poverty and ignorance, in order that those whose skin was white would have readily at hand a proof of their superiority, a proof patent and inclusive, accessible to the moron and the idiot as well as to the wise man and the genius. No matter how low a white man fell, he could always hold fast to the smug conviction that he was superior to two-thirds of the world's population, for those two-thirds were not white.

It made no difference how intelligent or talented my millions of brothers and I were, or how virtuously we lived. A curse like that of Judas was upon us, a mark of degradation fashioned with heavenly authority. There were white men who said Negroes had no souls, and who proved it by the Bible. Some of these now were approaching us, intent upon burning our house.

Theirs was a world of contrasts in values: superior and inferior, profit and loss, cooperative and noncooperative, civilized and aboriginal, white and black. If you were on the wrong end of the comparison, if you were inferior, if you were noncooperative, if you were aboriginal, if you were black, then you were marked for excision, expulsion, or extinction. I was a Negro; I was therefore that part of history which opposed the good, the just, and the enlightened. I was a Persian, falling before the hordes of Alexander. I was a Carthaginian, extinguished by the Legions of Rome. I was a Frenchman at Waterloo, an Anglo-Saxon at Hastings, a Confederate at Vicksburg. I was the defeated, wherever and whenever there was a defeat.

Yet as a boy there in the darkness amid the tightening fright, I knew the inexplicable thing—that my skin was as white as the skin of those who were coming at me.

The mob moved toward the lawn. I tried to aim my gun, wondering what it would feel like to kill a man. Suddenly there was a volley of shots. The mob hesitated, stopped. Some friends of my father's had barricaded themselves in a two-story brick building just below our house. It was they who had fired. Some of the mobsmen, still bloodthirsty, shouted, "Let's go get the nigger." Others, afraid now for their safety, held back. Our friends, noting the hesitation, fired another volley. The mob broke and retreated up Houston Street.

In the quiet that followed I put my gun aside and tried to relax. But a tension different from anything I had ever known possessed me. I was gripped by the knowledge of my identity, and in the depths of my soul I was vaguely aware that I was glad of it. I was sick with loathing for the hatred which had flared before me that night and come so close to making me a killer; but I was glad I was not one of those who hated; I was glad I was not one of those made sick and murderous by pride. I was glad I was not one of those whose story is in the history of the world, a record of bloodshed, rapine, and pillage. I was glad my mind and spirit were part of the races that had not fully awakened, and who therefore had still before them the opportunity to write a record of virtue as a memorandum to Armageddon.

It was all just a feeling then, inarticulate and melancholy, yet reassuring in the way that death and sleep are reassuring, and I have clung to it now for nearly half a century.

2   CHICAGO 1919

During and immediately after World War I, city after city experienced violent outbreaks against Negroes. The most bloody was probably that at East St. Louis, Illinois, in July of 1917, which was less of a riot than a massacre. In 1919, riots occurred in Washington, D.C., Chicago, Omaha, and other cities. After a horrible outbreak in Tulsa, Oklahoma, in June of 1921, the epidemic of this sort of urban racial violence subsided. The worst riot in 1919, and the one most extensively studied, was that in Chicago. The following summary and recommendations were prepared by a commission appointed after the riot to study conditions of the Negro in Chicago.

From The Chicago Commission on Race Relations, The Negro in Chicago: A Study of Race Relations and a Race Riot (*Chicago: The University of Chicago Press, 1922*), *pp. 595–98, 602, 640–49.*

In July, 1919, a race riot involving whites and Negroes occurred in Chicago. For some time thoughtful citizens, white and Negro, had sensed increasing tension, but, having no local precedent of riot and wholesale bloodshed, had neither prepared themselves for it nor taken steps to prevent it. The collecting of arms by members of both races was known to the authorities, and it was evident that this was in preparation for aggression as well as for self-defense.

Several minor clashes preceded the riot. On July 3, 1917, a white saloon-keeper who, according to the coroner's physician, died of heart trouble, was incorrectly reported in the press to have been killed by a Negro. That evening a party of young white men riding in an automobile fired upon a group of Negroes at Fifty-third and Federal Streets. In July and August of the same year recruits from the Great Lakes Naval Training Station clashed frequently with Negroes, each side accusing the other of being the aggressor.

Gangs of white "toughs," made up largely of the membership of so-called "athletic clubs" from the neighborhood between Roosevelt Road and Sixty-third Street, Wentworth Avenue and the city limits—a district contiguous to the neighborhood of the largest Negro settlement—were a constant menace to Negroes who traversed sections of the territory going to and returning from work. The activities of these gangs and "athletic clubs" became bolder in the spring of 1919, and on the night of June 21, five weeks before the riot, two wanton murders of Negroes occurred, those of Sanford Harris and Joseph Robinson. Harris returning to his home on Dearborn Street, about 11:30 at night, passed a group of young white men. They threatened him and he ran. He had gone but a short distance when one of the group shot him. He died soon afterward. Policemen who came on the scene made no arrests, even when the assailant was pointed out by a white woman witness of the murder. On the same evening Robinson, a Negro laborer, forty-seven years of age, was attacked while returning from work by a gang of white "roughs" at Fifty-fifth Street and Princeton Avenue, apparently without provocation, and stabbed to death.

Negroes were greatly incensed over these murders, but their leaders, joined by many friendly whites, tried to allay their fears and counseled patience.

After the killing of Harris and Robinson notices were conspicuously posted on the South Side that an effort would be made to "get all the niggers on July 4th." The notices called for help from sympathizers.

Negroes in turn whispered around the warning to prepare for a riot; and they did prepare.

Since the riot in East St. Louis, July 4, 1917, there had been others in different parts of the country which evidenced a widespread lack of restraint in mutual antipathies and suggested further resorts to lawlessness. Riots and race clashes occurred in Chester, Pennsylvania; Longview, Texas; Coatesville, Pennsylvania; Washington, D.C.; and Norfolk, Virginia, before the Chicago riot.

Aside from general lawlessness and disastrous riots that preceded the riot here discussed, there were other factors which may be mentioned briefly here. In Chicago considerable unrest had been occasioned in industry by increasing competition between white and Negro laborers following a sudden increase in the Negro population due to the migration of Negroes from the South. This increase developed a housing crisis. The Negroes overran the hitherto recognized area of Negro residence, and when they took houses in adjoining neighborhoods friction ensued. In the two years just preceding the riot, twenty-seven Negro dwellings were wrecked by bombs thrown by unidentified persons.

STORY OF THE RIOT

Sunday afternoon, July 27, 1919, hundreds of white and Negro bathers crowded the lake-front beaches at Twenty-sixth and Twenty-ninth Streets. This is the eastern boundary of the thickest Negro residence area. At Twenty-sixth Street Negroes were in great majority; at Twenty-ninth Street there were more whites. An imaginary line in the water separating the two beaches had been generally observed by the two races. Under the prevailing relations, aided by wild rumors and reports, this line served virtually as a challenge to either side to cross it. Four Negroes who attempted to enter the water from the "white" side were driven away by the whites. They returned with more Negroes, and there followed a series of attacks with stones, first one side gaining the advantage, then the other.

Eugene Williams, a Negro boy of seventeen, entered the water from the side used by Negroes and drifted across the line supported by a railroad tie. He was observed by the crowd on the beach and promptly became a target for stones. He suddenly released the tie, went down and was drowned. Guilt was immediately placed on Stauber, a young white man, by Negro witnesses who declared that he threw the fatal stone.[1]

White and Negro men dived for the boy without result. Negroes demanded that the policeman present arrest Stauber. He refused; and at this crucial moment arrested a Negro on a white man's complaint.

---

[1] The coroner's jury found that Williams had drowned from fear of stone-throwing which kept him from the shore.

Negroes then attacked the officer. These two facts, the drowning and the refusal of the policeman to arrest Stauber, together marked the beginning of the riot.

Two hours after the drowning, a Negro, James Crawford, fired into a group of officers summoned by the policeman at the beach and was killed by a Negro policeman. Reports and rumors circulated rapidly, and new crowds began to gather. Five white men were injured in clashes near the beach. As darkness came Negroes in white districts to the west suffered severely. Between 9:00 P.M. and 3:00 A.M. twenty-seven Negroes were beaten, seven stabbed, and four shot. Monday morning was quiet, and Negroes went to work as usual.

Returning from work in the afternoon many Negroes were attacked by white ruffians. Street-car routes, especially at transfer points, were the centers of lawlessness. Trolleys were pulled from the wires, and Negro passengers were dragged into the street, beaten, stabbed, and shot. The police were powerless to cope with these numerous assaults. During Monday, four Negro men and one white assailant were killed, and thirty Negroes were severely beaten in street-car clashes. Four white men were killed, six stabbed, five shot, and nine severely beaten. It was rumored that the white occupants of the Angelus Building at Thirty-fifth Street and Wabash Avenue had shot a Negro. Negroes gathered about the building. The white tenants sought police protection, and one hundred policemen, mounted and on foot, responded. In a clash with the mob the police killed four Negroes and injured many.

Raids into the Negro residence area then began. Automobiles sped through the streets, the occupants shooting at random. Negroes retaliated by "sniping" from ambush. At midnight surface and elevated car service was discontinued because of a strike for wage increases, and thousands of employees were cut off from work.

On Tuesday, July 29, Negro men en route on foot to their jobs through hostile territory were killed. White soldiers and sailors in uniform, aided by civilians, raided the "Loop" business section, killing two Negroes and beating and robbing several others. Negroes living among white neighbors in Englewood, far to the south, were driven from their homes, their household goods were stolen, and their houses were burned or wrecked. On the West Side an Italian mob, excited by a false rumor that an Italian girl had been shot by a Negro, killed Joseph Lovings, a Negro.

Wednesday night at 10:30 Mayor Thompson yielded to pressure and asked the help of the three regiments of militia which had been stationed in nearby armories during the most severe rioting, awaiting the call. They immediately took up positions throughout the South Side. A rainfall Wednesday night and Thursday kept many people in their homes, and by Friday the rioting had abated. On Saturday incendiary fires burned forty-nine houses in the immigrant neighborhood west of the Stock Yards.

Nine hundred and forty-eight people, mostly Lithuanians, were made homeless, and the property loss was about $250,000. Responsibility for the fires was never fixed.

The total casualties of this reign of terror were thirty-eight deaths—fifteen white, twenty-three Negro—and 537 people injured. Forty-one per cent of the reported clashes occurred in the white neighborhood near the Stock Yards between the south branch of the Chicago River and Fifty-fifth Street, Wentworth Avenue and the city limits, and 34 per cent in the "Black Belt" between Twenty-second and Thirty-ninth Streets, Wentworth Avenue and Lake Michigan. Others were scattered.

·   ·   ·

The riot was merely a symptom of serious and profound disorders lying beneath the surface of race relations in Chicago. The study of the riot, therefore, as to its interlocking provocations and causes, required a study of general race relations that made possible so serious and sudden an outbreak. Thus to understand the riot and guard against another, the Commission probed systematically into the principal phases of race contact and sought accurate information on matters which in the past have been influenced by dangerous speculation; and on the basis of its discoveries certain suggestions to the community are made.

·   ·   ·

THE RECOMMENDATIONS OF THE COMMISSION

1. We recommend that the police and militia work out, at the earliest possible date, a detailed plan for joint action in the control of race riots.

2. In accordance with such a plan, and in the event of race rioting, we specifically recommend: (a) that the militia, white and Negro, be promptly mobilized at the beginning of the outbreak; (b) that police and deputy sheriffs and militia, white and Negro, be so distributed as adequately to protect both races in white and Negro neighborhoods and to avoid the gross inequalities of protection which, in the riot of 1919, permitted widespread depredations, including murder, against Negroes in white neighborhoods, and attacks in Negro neighborhoods by invading white hoodlums; (c) that the police and militia be stationed with special reference to main street-car lines and transfer points used by Negroes in getting to and from work; (d) that substantial assurance be given of adequate and equal protection by all agencies of law enforcement, thus removing the incentive to arm in self-defense; (e) that in the appointment of special peace officers there shall be no discrimination against Negroes; (f) that all rioters, white and Negro, be arrested without race discrimination; (g) that all reports and complaints of neglect of duty or participation

in rioting by police, deputy sheriffs, or militia be promptly investigated and the offenders promptly punished; (*h*) that all persons arrested in connection with rioting be systematically booked on distinct charges showing such connection, in order to avoid the confusion and evasions of justice following the riot of 1919.

3. We recommend that, without regard to color, all persons arrested in connection with rioting be promptly tried and the guilty speedily punished. . . .

5. The testimony of court officials before the Commission and its investigations indicate that Negroes are more commonly arrested, subjected to police identification, and convicted than white offenders, that on similar evidence they are generally held and convicted on more serious charges, and that they are given longer sentences. . . . We recommend to the police, state's attorney, judges, and juries that they consider these conditions in the effort to deal fairly (and without discrimination) with all persons charged with crime.

6. We recommend that, in order to encourage respect for law by both Negroes and whites, the courts discountenance the facetiousness which is too common in dealing with cases in which Negroes are involved.

7. We recommend that the police, state's attorney, and other authorities promptly rid the Negro residence areas of vice resorts, whose present exceptional prevalence in such areas is due to official laxity.

8. We recommend better cooperation between the city and park police in and near parks, bathing-beaches, and other public recreation places, especially where there has been or is likely to be race friction; and in the speedy punishment of persons guilty of stoning houses, molesting individuals, or committing other depredations calculated to arouse race antagonism. . . .

13. We recommend that the authorities exercise their powers to condemn and raze all houses unfit for human habitation, many of which the Commission has found to exist in the Negro residence areas on the South and West sides.

14. We recommend better enforcement of health and sanitary laws and regulations in the care, repair, and upkeep of streets and alleys and the collection and disposal of rubbish and garbage in areas of Negro residence, where the Commission has found these matters to be shamefully neglected. . . .

16. We recommend that in the areas where the main part of the Negro population lives, and where elementary-school accommodations are notably deficient, buildings, equipment, and teaching forces be provided which shall be at least equal to the average standard for the city, in order that the present conditions of overcrowding, arrangement of pupils in shifts, and the assignment of too large classes to teachers may be remedied.

17. We recommend the establishment of night schools and community

centers in sections of the city not now adequately provided with such facilities.

18. Having found that many Negro children who quit school at an early age, as in the case of similar white children, appear later as criminals and delinquents, we urge strict enforcement of regulations as to working permits for such children, and we especially recommend that truant officers give attention to school attendance by the children of Negro families migrating here from the South.

19. Since the attitude of principals and teachers vitally influences the relations of white and Negro children in the public schools, we recommend that special care be exercised in appointing principals and teachers who have a sympathetic and intelligent interest in promoting good race relations in the schools. . . .

31. We recommend as of special importance that a permanent local body representing both races be charged with investigating situations likely to produce clashes, with collecting and disseminating information tending to preserve the peace and allay unfounded fears, with bringing sound public sentiment to bear upon the settlement of racial disputes, and with promoting the spirit of interracial tolerance and cooperation. . . .

33. Our inquiry has shown that insufficiency in amount and quality of housing is an all-important factor in Chicago's race problem; there must be more and better housing to accommodate the great increase in Negro population which was at the rate of 148 per cent from 1910 to 1920. This situation will be made worse by methods tending toward forcible segregation or exclusion of Negroes, such as the circulation of threatening statements and propaganda by organizations or persons to prevent Negroes from living in certain areas, and the lawless and perilous bombing of houses occupied by Negroes or by whites suspected of encouraging Negro residence in the district.

We therefore recommend that all white citizens energetically discourage these futile, pernicious, and lawless practices, and either cooperate in or start movements to solve the housing problem by constructive and not destructive methods. . . .

43. We have found that in struggles between capital and labor Negro workers are in a position dangerous to themselves and to peaceful relations between the races, whether the issues involve their use by employers to undermine wage standards or break strikes, or efforts by organized labor to keep them out of certain trades while refusing to admit them to membership in the unions in such trades. We feel that unnecessary racial bitterness is provoked by such treatment of Negro workers, that racial prejudice is played upon by both parties, and that through such practices injury comes, not alone to Negroes, but to employers and labor organizations as well.

We therefore recommend to employers that they deal with Negroes as workmen on the same plane as white workers; and to labor unions that they admit Negroes to full membership whenever they apply for it and possess the qualifications required of white workers. . . .

45. In view of the limited field of employment within which Negroes are restricted we recommend that employers in all lines enlarge that field and permit Negroes an equal chance with whites to enter all positions for which they are qualified by efficiency and merit. . . .

46. We have found that Negroes are denied equal opportunity with whites for advancement and promotion where they are employed. As a measure of justice we urge that Negroes be employed, advanced, and promoted according to their capacities and proved merit. We call to the attention of those concerned the high qualifications of many Negro workers in sleeping-car and dining-car service, and recommend that when they deserve it and the opportunity offers, they be made eligible for promotion to positions as conductors and stewards. . . .

57. We point out that Negroes are entitled by law to the same treatment as other persons in restaurants, theaters, stores, and other places of public accommodation, and we urge that owners and managers of such places govern their policies and actions and their employees accordingly.

3 "IF WE MUST DIE"
CLAUDE MC KAY DEFIES THE MOB

*No one expressed the spirit of defiance in the face of the anti-Negro
violence more effectively than Claude McKay in the poem reprinted here.
A native of Jamaica in the British West Indies, McKay became a
resident of New York City and a major figure of the Harlem
Renaissance of the 1920s.*

Claude McKay, "If We Must Die." From Selected Poems of
Claude McKay (*New York: Bookman Associates, Inc., 1953), p. 36.
Reprinted by permission of Twayne Publishers, Inc.*

IF WE MUST DIE

If we must die, let it not be like hogs
Hunted and penned in an inglorious spot,
While round us bark the mad and hungry dogs,
Making their mock at our accursed lot.
If we must die, O let us nobly die,
So that our precious blood may not be shed
In vain; then even the monsters we defy
Shall be constrained to honor us though dead!
O kinsmen! we must meet the common foe!
Though far outnumbered let us show us brave,
And for their thousand blows deal one deathblow!
What though before us lies the open grave?
Like men we'll face the murderous, cowardly pack,
Pressed to the wall, dying, but fighting back!

4 POLICE BRUTALITY IN DETROIT: 1943

Although a serious riot occurred in Harlem in March of 1935, the next major epidemic of urban racial violence broke out in 1943 following the influx of Negroes to the cities that began during World War II. The bloodiest riot was in Detroit in June of 1943, resulting in the deaths of some twenty-five Negroes and nine whites. Thurgood Marshall, the first Negro to be appointed to the United States Supreme Court, was then chief counsel for the NAACP. In this selection, written shortly after the outbreak, he condemns the action of the Detroit police.

From Thurgood Marshall, "The Gestapo in Detroit," Crisis 50 (August, 1943): 232–33, 246–47. Reprinted by permission of The Crisis Publishing Company, Inc.

Riots are usually the result of many underlying causes, yet no single factor is more important than the attitude and efficiency of the police. When disorder starts, it is either stopped quickly or permitted to spread into serious proportions, depending upon the actions of the local police.

Much of the blood spilled in the Detroit riot is on the hands of the Detroit police department. In the past the Detroit police have been guilty of both inefficiency and an attitude of prejudice against Negroes. Of course, there are several individual exceptions. . . .

In the June riot of this year, the police ran true to form. The trouble reached riot proportions because the police once again enforced the law with an unequal hand. They used "persuasion" rather than firm action with white rioters, while against Negroes they used the ultimate in force: night sticks, revolvers, riot guns, sub-machine guns, and deer guns. As a result, 25 of the 34 persons killed were Negroes. Of the latter, 17 were killed by police.

The excuse of the police department for the disproportionate number of Negroes killed is that the majority of them were shot while committing felonies: namely, the looting of stores on Hastings Street. On the other hand, the crimes of arson and felonious assaults are also felonies. It is true that some Negroes were looting stores and were shot while committing these crimes. It is equally true that white persons were turning over and burning automobiles on Woodward Avenue. This is arson. Others were beating Negroes with iron pipes, clubs, and rocks. This is felonious assault. Several Negroes were stabbed. This is assault with intent to murder.

All these crimes are matters of record; many were committed in the presence of police officers, several on the pavement around the City Hall. Yet the record remains: Negroes killed by police—17; white persons killed by police—none. The entire record, both of the riot killings and of previous disturbances, reads like the story of the Nazi Gestapo. . . .

SUNDAY NIGHT ON BELLE ISLE

Belle Isle is a municipal recreation park where thousands of white and Negro war workers and their families go on Sundays for their outings. There had been isolated instances of racial friction in the past. On Sunday night, June 20, there was trouble between a group of white and Negro people. The disturbance was under control by midnight. During the time of the disturbance and after it was under control, the police searched the automobiles of all Negroes and searched the Negroes as well. They did not search the white people. One Negro who was to be inducted into the army the following week was arrested because another person in the car had a small pen knife. This youth was later sentenced to 90 days in jail before his family could locate him. Many Negroes were arrested during this period and rushed to local police stations. At the very beginning the police demonstrated that they would continue to handle racial disorders by searching, beating and arresting Negroes while using mere persuasion on white people.

THE RIOT SPREADS

A short time after midnight disorder broke out in a white neighborhood near the Roxy theatre on Woodward Avenue. The Roxy is an all-night theatre attended by white and Negro patrons. Several Negroes were beaten and other were forced to remain in the theatre for lack of police protection. The rumor spread among the white people that a Negro had raped a white woman on Belle Isle and that the Negroes were rioting.

At about the same time a rumor spread around Hastings and Adams streets in the Negro area that white sailors had thrown a Negro woman and her baby into the lake at Belle Isle and that the police were beating Negroes. This rumor was also repeated by an unidentified Negro at one of the night spots. Some Negroes began to attack white persons in the area. The police immediately began to use their sticks and revolvers against them. The Negroes began to break out the windows of stores of white merchants on Hastings Street.

The interesting thing is that when the windows in the stores on Hastings Street were first broken, there was no looting. An officer of the Merchants'

Association walked the length of Hastings Street, starting 7 o'clock Monday morning, and noticed that none of the stores with broken windows had been looted. It is thus clear that the original breaking of windows was not for the purpose of looting.

Throughout Monday the police, instead of placing men in front of the stores to protect them from looting, contented themselves with driving up and down Hastings Street from time to time, stopping in front of the stores. The usual procedure was to jump out of the squad cars with drawn revolvers and riot guns to shoot whoever might be in the store. The policemen would then tell the Negro bystanders to "run and not look back." On several occasions, persons running were shot in the back. In other instances, bystanders were clubbed by police. To the police, all Negroes on Hastings Street were "looters." This included war workers returning from work. There is no question that many Negroes were guilty of looting, just as there is always looting during earthquakes or as there was when English towns were bombed by the Germans.

CARS DETOURED INTO MOBS

Woodward Avenue is one of the main thoroughfares of the city of Detroit. Small groups of white people began to rove up and down Woodward beating Negroes, stoning cars containing Negroes, stopping street cars and yanking Negroes from them, and stabbing and shooting Negroes. In no case did the police do more than try to "reason" with these mobs, many of which were, at this stage, quite small. The police did not draw their revolvers or riot guns, and never used any force to disperse these mobs. As a result of this, the mobs got larger and bolder and even attacked Negroes on the pavement of the City Hall in demonstration not only of their contempt for Negroes, but of their contempt for law and order as represented by the municipal government.

During this time, Mayor Jeffries was in his office in the City Hall with the door locked and the window shade drawn. The use of night sticks or the drawing of revolvers would have dispersed these white groups and saved the lives of many Negroes. It would not have been necessary to shoot, but it would have been sufficient to threaten to shoot into the white mobs. The use of a fire hose would have dispersed many of the groups. None of these things was done and the disorder took on the proportions of a major riot. The responsibility rests with the Detroit police. . . .

While investigating the riot, we obtained many affidavits from Negroes concerning police brutality during the riot. It is impossible to include the facts of all of these affidavits. However, typical instances may be cited. A Negro soldier in uniform who had recently been released from the army with a medical discharge, was on his way down Brush Street Monday morning, toward a theatre on Woodward Avenue. This soldier was not aware of the fact that the riot was still going on. While in the Negro neighborhood on Brush Street, he reached a corner where a squad car drove up and discharged several policemen with drawn revolvers who announced to a small group on the corner to run and not look back. Several of the Negroes who did not move quite fast enough for the police were struck with night sticks and revolvers. The soldier was yanked from behind by one policeman and struck in the head with a blunt instrument and knocked to the ground, where he remained in a stupor. The police then returned to their squad car and drove off. A Negro woman in the block noticed the entire incident from her window, and she rushed out with a cold, damp towel to bind the soldier's head. She then hailed two Negro postal employees who carried the soldier to a hospital where his life was saved. . . .

In addition to the many cases of one-sided enforcement of the law by the police, there are two glaring examples of criminal aggression against innocent Negro citizens and workers by members of the Michigan state police and Detroit police.

SHOOTING IN YMCA

On the night of June 22 at about 10 o'clock, some of the residents of the St. Antoine Branch of the Y.M.C.A. were returning to the dormitory. Several were on their way home from the Y.W.C.A. across the street. State police were searching some other Negroes on the pavement of the Y.M.C.A. when two of the Y.M.C.A. residents were stopped and searched for weapons. After none was found they were allowed to proceed to the building. Just as the last of the Y.M.C.A. men was about to enter the building, he heard someone behind him yell what sounded to him like, "Hi, Ridley." (Ridley is also a resident of the Y.) Another resident said he heard someone yell what sounded to him like "Heil, Hitler."

A state policeman, Ted Anders, jumped from his car with his revolver drawn, ran to the steps of the Y.M.C.A. put one foot on the bottom step and fired through the outside door. Immediately after firing the shot he entered the building. Other officers followed. Julian Witherspoon, who had just entered the building, was lying on the floor, shot in the side by the bullet that was fired through the outside door. There had been no show of violence or weapons of any kind by anyone in or around the Y.M.C.A.

The officers with drawn revolvers ordered all those residents of the Y.M.C.A. who were in the lobby of their building, to raise their hands in the air and line up against the wall like criminals. During all this time these men were called "black b—— and monkeys," and other vile names by the officers. At least one man was struck; another was forced to throw his lunch on the floor. All the men in the lobby were searched.

The desk clerk was also forced to line up. The officers then went behind the desk and into the private offices and searched everything. The officers also made the clerk open all locked drawers, threatening to shoot him if he did not do so.

Witherspoon was later removed to the hospital and has subsequently been released.

VERNOR APARTMENT SIEGE

On the night of June 21 at about eight o'clock, a Detroit policeman was shot in the two hundred block of Vernor Highway, and his assailant, who was in a vacant lot, was, in turn, killed by another policeman. State and city policemen then began to attack the apartment building at 290 E. Vernor Highway, which was fully occupied by tenants. Searchlights were thrown on the building and machine guns, revolvers, rifles, and deer guns were fired indiscriminately into all of the occupied apartments facing the outside. Tenants of the building were forced to fall to the floor and remain there in order to save their lives. Later slugs from machine guns, revolvers, rifles, and deer guns were dug from the inside walls of many of the apartments. Tear gas was shot into the building and all the tenants were forced out into the streets with their hands up in the air at the point of drawn guns.

State and city policemen went into the building and forced out all the tenants who were not driven out by tear gas. The tenants were all lined up against the walls, men and women alike, and forced to remain in this position for some time. The men were searched for weapons. During this time these people were called every type of vile name and men and women were cursed and threatened. Many men were struck by policemen.

While the tenants were lined up in the street, the apartments were forcibly entered. Locks and doors were broken. All the apartments were ransacked. Clothing and other articles were thrown around on the floor. All of these acts were committed by policemen. Most of the tenants reported that money, jewelry, whiskey, and other items of personal property were missing when they were permitted to return to their apartments after midnight. State and city police had been in possession of the building in the meantime.

Many of these apartments were visited shortly after these events. They resembled part of a battlefield. Affidavits from most of the tenants and lists of property destroyed and missing are available.

Although a white man was seen on the roof of an apartment house up the street from the Vernor apartments with a rifle in his hand, no effort was made to either search that building or its occupants. After the raid on the Vernor apartments, the police used as their excuse the statement that policeman Lawrence A. Adams had been shot by a sniper from the Vernor apartments, and that for that reason, they attacked the building and its occupants. However, in a story released by the police department on July 2 after the death of Patrolman Lawrence A. Adams, it was reported that "The shot that felled Adams was fired by Homer Edison, 28 years old, of 502 Montcalm, from the shadows of a parking lot. Edison, armed with a shot gun, was shot to death by Adams' partner." This is merely another example of the clumsy and obvious subterfuges used by the police department in an effort to cover up their total disregard for the rights of Negroes. . . .

This record by the Detroit police demonstrates once more what all Negroes know only too well: that nearly all police departments limit their conception of checking racial disorders to surrounding, arresting, maltreating, and shooting Negroes. Little attempt is made to check the activities of whites.

The certainty of Negroes that they will not be protected by police, but instead attacked by them is a contributing factor to racial tensions leading to overt acts. The first item on the agenda of any group seeking to prevent rioting would seem to be a critical study of the police department of the community, its record in handling Negroes, something of the background of its personnel, and the plans of its chief officers for meeting possible racial disorders.

5 TOWARD TWO SOCIETIES? THE KERNER COMMISSION REPORT

For ten years after the Supreme Court's 1954 decision against school segregation, the major attention of the civil rights movement was on the South. For the population of the ever-growing black ghettos, however, the problems of slums, unemployment, bad schools—the whole way of life— remained much as before. Certainly there were no improvements commensurate with the expectations that had been raised by the civil rights struggle. In July and August of 1964, the black ghettos of Harlem, Rochester, Jersey City, Chicago, and Philadelphia exploded in rapid succession. A year later, a far worse upheaval took place in the Watts district of Los Angeles. Sporadic violence occurred in the summer of 1966, and conflicts in Newark and Detroit in July of 1967 resulted in sixty-three deaths. These outbreaks were different from the typical massacres that had taken place earlier in the century in the extent to which Negroes caused tremendous amounts of property

*damage as they vented their rage against the symbols of white
oppression. In July of 1967, President Johnson appointed a commission
headed by Governor Otto Kerner of Illinois to study this violence. The
following selection, taken from the commission's summary, is a grim
warning of the degree to which American society was endangered by its
present course.*

From Report of the National Advisory Commission on Civil
Disorders (*Washington, D.C.: U.S. Government Printing Office,
1968*), *pp. 1–5, 10–11.*

INTRODUCTION

The summer of 1967 again brought racial disorders to American cities, and with them shock, fear, and bewilderment to the Nation.

The worst came during a 2-week period in July, first in Newark and then in Detroit. Each set off a chain reaction in neighboring communities.

On July 28, 1967, the President of the United States established this Commission and directed us to answer three basic questions:

What happened?

Why did it happen?

What can be done to prevent it from happening again?

To respond to these questions, we have undertaken a broad range of studies and investigations. We have visited the riot cities; we have heard many witnesses; we have sought the counsel of experts across the country.

This is our basic conclusion: Our Nation is moving toward two societies, one black, one white—separate and unequal.

Reaction to last summer's disorders has quickened the movement and deepened the division. Discrimination and segregation have long permeated much of American life; they now threaten the future of every American.

This deepening racial division is not inevitable. The movement apart can be reversed. Choice is still possible. Our principal task is to define that choice and to press for a national resolution.

To pursue our present course will involve the continuing polarization of the American community and, ultimately, the destruction of basic democratic values.

The alternative is not blind repression or capitulation to lawlessness. It is the realization of common opportunities for all within a single society.

This alternative will require a commitment to national action—compassionate, massive, and sustained, backed by the resources of the most powerful and the richest nation on this earth. From every American it will require new attitudes, new understanding, and, above all, new will.

The vital needs of the Nation must be met; hard choices must be made, and, if necessary, new taxes enacted.

Violence cannot build a better society. Disruption and disorder nourish repression, not justice. They strike at the freedom of every citizen. The community cannot—it will not—tolerate coercion and mob rule.

Violence and destruction must be ended—in the streets of the ghetto and in the lives of people.

Segregation and poverty have created in the racial ghetto a destructive environment totally unknown to most white Americans.

What white Americans have never fully understood—but what the Negro can never forget—is that white society is deeply implicated in the ghetto. White institutions created it, white institutions maintain it, and white society condones it.

It is time now to turn with all the purpose at our command to the major unfinished business of this Nation. It is time to adopt strategies for action that will produce quick and visible progress. It is time to make good the promises of American democracy to all citizens—urban and rural, white and black, Spanish-surname, American Indian, and every minority group.

Our recommendations embrace three basic principles:

> To mount programs on a scale equal to the dimension of the problems;
> To aim these programs for high impact in the immediate future in order to close the gap between promise and performance;
> To undertake new initiatives and experiments that can change the system of failure and frustration that now dominates the ghetto and weakens our society.

These programs will require unprecedented levels of funding and performance, but they neither probe deeper nor demand more than the problems which called them forth. There can be no higher priority for national action and no higher claim on the Nation's conscience.

We issue this report now, 5 months before the date called for by the President. Much remains that can be learned. Continued study is essential.

As Commissioners we have worked together with a sense of the greatest urgency and have sought to compose whatever differences exist among us. Some differences remain. But the gravity of the problem and the pressing need for action are too clear to allow further delay in the issuance of this report. . . .

Patterns of Disorder

The "typical" riot did not take place. The disorders of 1967 were unusual, irregular, complex, and unpredictable social processes. Like most human events, they did not unfold in an orderly sequence. However, an analysis of our survey information leads to some conclusions about the riot process.

In general:

The civil disorders of 1967 involved Negroes acting against local symbols of white American society, authority, and property in Negro neighborhoods—rather than against white persons.

Of 164 disorders reported during the first nine months of 1967, eight (5 percent) were major in terms of violence and damage; 33 (20 percent) were serious but not major; 123 (75 percent) were minor and undoubtedly would not have received national attention as riots had the Nation not been sensitized by the more serious outbreaks.

In the 75 disorders studied by a Senate subcommittee, 83 deaths were reported. Eighty-two percent of the deaths and more than half the injuries occurred in Newark and Detroit. About 10 percent of the dead and 36 percent of the injured were public employees, primarily law officers and firemen. The overwhelming majority of the persons killed or injured in all the disorders were Negro civilians.

Initial damage estimates were greatly exaggerated. In Detroit, newspaper damage estimates at first ranged from $200 to $500 million; the highest recent estimate is $45 million. In Newark, early estimates ranged from $15 to $25 million. A month later damage was estimated at $10.2 million, 80 percent in inventory losses.

In the 24 disorders in 23 cities which we surveyed:

The final incident before the outbreak of disorder, and the initial violence itself, generally took place in the evening or at night at a place in which it was normal for many people to be on the streets.

Violence usually occurred almost immediately following the occurrence of the final precipitating incident, and then escalated rapidly. With but few exceptions, violence subsided during the day, and flared rapidly again at night. The night-day cycles continued through the early period of the major disorders.

Disorder generally began with rock and bottle throwing and window breaking. Once store windows were broken, looting usually followed.

Disorder did not erupt as a result of a single "triggering" or "precipitating" incident. Instead, it was generated out of an increasingly disturbed social atmosphere, in which typically a series of tension-heightening incidents over a period of weeks or months became linked in the minds of many in the Negro community with a reservoir of underlying grievances. At some point in the mounting tension, a further incident—in itself often routine or trivial—became the breaking point and the tension spilled over into violence.

"Prior" incidents, which increased tensions and ultimately led to violence, were police actions in almost half the cases; police actions were "final" incidents before the outbreak of violence in 12 of the 24 surveyed disorders.

No particular control tactic was successful in every situation. The varied effectiveness of control techniques emphasizes the need for advance training, planning, adequate intelligence systems, and knowledge of the ghetto community.

Negotiations between Negroes—including young militants as well as older Negro leaders—and white officials concerning "terms of peace" occurred during virtually all the disorders surveyed. In many cases, these negotiations involved discussion of underlying grievances as well as the handling of the disorder by control authorities.

The typical rioter was a teenager or young adult, a life-long resident of the city in which he rioted, a high school dropout; he was, nevertheless, somewhat better educated than his nonrioting Negro neighbor, and was usually under-employed or employed in a menial job. He was proud of his race, extremely hostile to both whites and middle-class Negroes and, although informed about politics, highly distrustful of the political system.

A Detroit survey revealed that approximately 11 per cent of the total residents of two riot areas admitted participation in the rioting, 20 to 25 per cent identified themselves as "bystanders," over 16 per cent identified themselves as "counterrioters" who urged rioters to "cool it," and the remaining 48 to 53 per cent said they were at home or elsewhere and did not participate. In a survey of Negro males between the ages of 15 and 35 residing in the disturbance area in Newark, about 45 per cent identified themselves as rioters, and about 55 per cent as "noninvolved."

Most rioters were young Negro males. Nearly 53 percent of arrestees were between 15 and 24 years of age; nearly 81 percent between 15 and 35.

In Detroit and Newark about 74 percent of the rioters were brought up in the North. In contrast, of the noninvolved, 36 percent in Detroit and 52 percent in Newark were brought up in the North.

What the rioters appeared to be seeking was fuller participation in the social order and the material benefits enjoyed by the majority of American citizens. Rather than rejecting the American system, they were anxious to obtain a place for themselves in it.

Numerous Negro counterrioters walked the streets urging rioters to "cool it." The typical counterrioter was better educated and had higher income than either the rioter or the noninvolved.

The proportion of Negroes in local government was substantially smaller than the Negro proportion of population. Only three of the 20 cities studied had more than one Negro legislator; none had ever had a Negro mayor or city manager. In only four cities did Negroes hold other important policy-making positions or serve as heads of municipal departments.

Although almost all cities had some sort of formal grievance mechanism for handling citizen complaints, this typically was regarded by Negroes as ineffective and was generally ignored.

Although specific grievances varied from city to city, at least 12 deeply held grievances can be identified and ranked into three levels of relative intensity:

First level of intensity:

1. Police practices
2. Unemployment and underemployment
3. Inadequate housing

Second level of intensity:

4. Inadequate education
5. Poor recreation facilities and programs
6. Ineffectiveness of the political structure and grievance mechanisms

Third level of intensity:

7. Disrespectful white attitudes
8. Discriminatory administration of justice
9. Inadequacy of Federal programs
10. Inadequacy of municipal services
11. Discriminatory consumer and credit practices
12. Inadequate welfare programs

The results of a three-city survey of various Federal programs—manpower, education, housing, welfare and community action—indicate that, despite substantial expenditures, the number of persons assisted constituted only a fraction of those in need.

The background of disorder is often as complex and difficult to analyze as the disorder itself. But we find that certain general conclusions can be drawn:

Social and economic conditions in the riot cities constituted a clear pattern of severe disadvantage for Negroes compared with whites, whether the Negroes lived in the area where the riot took place or outside it. Negroes had completed fewer years of education and fewer had attended high school. Negroes were twice as likely to be unemployed and three times as likely to be in unskilled and service jobs. Negroes averaged 70 percent of the income earned by whites and were more than twice as likely to be living in poverty. Although housing cost Negroes relatively more, they had worse housing—three times as likely to be overcrowded and substandard. When compared to white suburbs, the relative disadvantage was even more pronounced.

A study of the aftermath of disorder leads to disturbing conclusions. We find that, despite the institution of some postriot programs:

Little basic change in the conditions underlying the outbreak of disorder has taken place. Actions to ameliorate Negro grievances have been limited and sporadic; with but few exceptions, they have not significantly reduced tensions.

In several cities, the principal official response has been to train and equip the police with more sophisticated weapons.

In several cities, increasing polarization is evident, with continuing breakdown of interracial communication, and growth of white segregationist or black separatist groups.

•　　•　　•

WHY DID IT HAPPEN?

The Basic Causes

In addressing the question "Why did it happen?" we shift our focus from the local to the national scene, from the particular events of the summer of 1967 to the factors within the society at large that created a mood of violence among many urban Negroes.

These factors are complex and interacting; they vary significantly in their effect from city to city and from year to year; and the consequences of one disorder, generating new grievances and new demands, become the causes of the next. Thus was created the "thicket of tension, conflicting evidence, and extreme opinions" cited by the President.

Despite these complexities, certain fundamental matters are clear. Of these, the most fundamental is the racial attitude and behavior of white Americans toward black Americans.

Race prejudice has shaped our history decisively; it now threatens to affect our future.

White racism is essentially responsible for the explosive mixture which has been accumulating in our cities since the end of World War II. Among the ingredients of this mixture are:

Pervasive discrimination and segregation in employment, education, and housing, which have resulted in the continuing exclusion of great numbers of Negroes from the benefits of economic progress.

Black in-migration and white exodus, which have produced the massive and growing concentrations of impoverished Negroes in our major cities, creating a growing crisis of deteriorating facilities and services and unmet human needs.

The black ghettos, where segregation and poverty converge on the young to destroy opportunity and enforce failure. Crime, drug addiction, dependency on welfare, and bitterness and resentment against society in general and white society in particular are the result.

At the same time, most whites and some Negroes outside the ghetto have prospered to a degree unparalleled in the history of civilization. Through television and other media, this affluence has been flaunted before the eyes of the Negro poor and the jobless ghetto youth.

Yet these facts alone cannot be said to have caused the disorders. Recently, other powerful ingredients have begun to catalyze the mixture.

Frustrated hopes are the residue of the unfulfilled expectations aroused by the great judicial and legislative victories of the civil rights movement and the dramatic struggle for equal rights in the South.

A climate that tends toward approval and encouragement of violence as a form of protest has been created by white terrorism directed against nonviolent protest; by the open defiance of law and Federal authority by state and local officials resisting desegregation; and by some protest groups engaging in civil disobedience who turn their backs on nonviolence, go beyond the constitutionally protected rights of petition and free assembly, and resort to violence to attempt to compel alteration of laws and policies with which they disagree.

The frustrations of powerlessness have led some Negroes to the conviction that there is no effective alternative to violence as a means of achieving redress of grievances, and of "moving the system." These frustrations are reflected in alienation and hostility toward the institutions of law and government and the white society which controls them, and in the reach toward racial consciousness and solidarity reflected in the slogan "Black Power."

A new mood has sprung up among Negroes, particularly among the young, in which self-esteem and enhanced racial pride are replacing apathy and submission to "the system."

The police are not merely a "spark" factor. To some Negroes police have come to symbolize white power, white racism, and white repression. And the fact is that many police do reflect and express these white attitudes. The atmosphere of hostility and cynicism is reinforced by a widespread belief among Negroes in the existence of police brutality and in a "double standard" of justice and protection—one for Negroes and one for whites.

To this point, we have attempted only to identify the prime components of the "explosive mixture." [We will now] seek to analyze them in the perspective of history. Their meaning, however, is clear:

In the summer of 1967, we have seen in our cities a chain reaction of racial violence. If we are heedless, none of us shall escape the consequences. . . .

The Future of the Cities

By 1985, the Negro population in central cities is expected to increase by 68 per cent to approximately 20.3 million. Coupled with the continued exodus of white families to the suburbs, this growth will produce majority Negro populations in many of the Nation's largest cities.

The future of these cities, and of their burgeoning Negro populations, is grim. Most new employment opportunities are being created in suburbs and outlying areas. This trend will continue unless important changes in public policy are made.

In prospect, therefore, is further deterioration of already inadequate municipal tax bases in the face of increasing demands for public services, and continuing unemployment and poverty among the urban Negro population:

Three choices are open to the Nation:

We can maintain present policies, continuing both the proportion of the Nation's resources now allocated to programs for the unemployed and the disadvantaged, and the inadequate and failing effort to achieve an integrated society.

We can adopt a policy of "enrichment" aimed at improving dramatically the quality of ghetto life while abandoning integration as a goal.

We can pursue integration by combining ghetto "enrichment" with policies which will encourage Negro movement out of central-city areas.

The first choice, continuance of present policies, has ominous consequences for our society. The share of the Nation's resources now allocated to programs for the disadvantaged is insufficient to arrest the deterioration of life in central city ghettos. Under such conditions, a rising proportion of Negroes may come to see in the deprivation and segregation they experience, a justification for violent protest, or for extending support to now isolated extremists who advocate civil disruption. Large-scale and continuing violence could result, followed by white retaliation, and, ultimately, the separation of the two communities in a garrison state.

Even if violence does not occur, the consequences are unacceptable. Development of a racially integrated society, extraordinarily difficult today, will be virtually impossible when the present black central-city population of 12.1 million has grown to almost 21 million.

To continue present policies is to make permanent the division of our country into two societies: one, largely Negro and poor, located in the central cities; the other, predominantly white and affluent, located in the suburbs and in outlying areas.

The second choice, ghetto enrichment coupled with abandonment of integration, is also unacceptable. It is another way of choosing a permanently divided country. Moreover, equality cannot be achieved under conditions of nearly complete separation. In a country where the economy, and particularly the resources of employment, are predominantly white, a policy of separation can only relegate Negroes to a permanently inferior economic status.

We believe that the only possible choice for America is the third—a policy which combines ghetto enrichment with programs designed to encourage integration of substantial numbers of Negroes into the society outside the ghetto.

Enrichment must be an important adjunct to integration, for no matter how ambitious or energetic the program, few Negroes now living in central cities can be quickly integrated. In the meantime, large-scale improvement in the quality of ghetto life is essential.

But this can be no more than an interim strategy. Programs must be developed which will permit substantial Negro movement out of the ghettos. The primary goal must be a single society, in which every citizen will be free to live and work according to his capabilities and desires, not his color.

VII   Politics and Protest

In the city the response of Negroes to their various grievances has varied widely from the seeking of redress through conventional political channels to the desperate and destructive acts of violence of the 1960s. Some aspects of the latter were described in the previous chapter. In the following selections three approaches may be discerned: the careful use of the ballot to bargain for desired objectives, an escape from the problem by emigrating to Africa, and the more recent call for "black power." There are some common elements to all three points of view. Thus the proper use of the vote is clearly one aspect of black power, and the racial pride emphasized in Garvey's back-to-Africa movement was close in spirit to the recent emphasis on blackness. While all three approaches have achieved something, none has yet succeeded in raising the quality of Negro life in the city, or in America at large, to the level that is the birthright of all Americans.

1 DUBOIS WARNS THE REPUBLICANS IN 1920

*The traditional loyalty of most black voters to the Republican Party
since Reconstruction was of little use in protecting or advancing the
status of the Negro population. Despite the Republican ascendancy from
the 1890s to 1913, Negroes in the South were robbed of their most
basic rights during those years by lynchings, segregation legislation,
disenfranchisement, and other forms of racial proscription, while in the
North they remained in a second-class status. Outside of the South,
however, they could vote, and as their numbers increased as a result
of the great migration, so did their potential political power. A
growing number of Negro leaders advised black voters to cast off their
traditional ties to the G.O.P. and to use their votes to bargain for
desired objectives regardless of party. W. E. B. DuBois'
recommendations for the 1920 election are given here.*

*From W. E. B. DuBois, "Republicans and the Black Voter," Nation
110 (June 5, 1920): 757–58.*

If we take as our basis the election of 1916 and assume that women will
vote, it would seem probable that the balance of power which will determine the way in which the electoral votes of eight pivotal States will be
cast will depend roughly upon the following number of voters: Illinois,
100,000; Indiana, 10,000; Kentucky, 60,000; Maryland, 40,000; Michigan, 90,000; New Jersey, 120,000; New York, 220,000; Ohio, 180,000.
The electoral votes of Connecticut, Delaware, Iowa, Kansas, Massachu-
setts, Minnesota, Missouri, Pennsylvania, and West Virginia may depend
on an equally narrow marginal group, and the decision in these seventeen
states will determine the election. Recently there has been a large migration of adult Negroes from the South. It seems probable, then, that in the
next election the number of Negroes eligible to vote will be: Illinois,
125,000; Michigan, 25,000; Indiana, 45,000; Kentucky, 150,000; Maryland, 150,000; New Jersey, 75,000; New York, 125,000; Ohio, 100,000.
If this estimate should prove true, then in the first mentioned four states,
the Negro voter easily holds the balance of power. In four others he might
hold the balance in a fairly close election. Moreover, he holds large power
and in many Congressional districts decisive power in the other nine states

mentioned. He could then, if he voted intelligently and with an eye single to his greatest political advantage, decide the election of 1920.

He could not only decide who would be President but more important, he could greatly influence the complexion of Congress. The present Senate has forty-seven Democrats and forty-nine Republicans, so that without the indicted Senator from Michigan the Republicans lead by one. Nine senators are to be elected from Iowa, Kansas, Ohio, Kentucky, Illinois, Maryland, Missouri, Indiana, and New York. The Negro vote might easily decide which party should control the Senate. The House Republican majority is forty-one, and Negroes by voting carefully in the forty-one Districts might easily cut down if not destroy it.

The reader will immediately say: This is all very well and would call for careful attention if the Negro voter were intelligent, experienced and determined. But he has a large percentage of illiteracy; he has had no political experience; and hitherto he has voted with his heart and not his head. We may, therefore, be sure that the Republicans are not losing much sleep over the Negro vote. They are saying that Wilson has made it impossible for any Negro to vote Democratic, and therefore there is nothing else for him to do but vote Republican. This calculation may be sound, but there are other considerations. First, the Negroes as a mass have done more thinking in the last four years than ever before. Second, they have long-standing grievances against the Republican Party, and it cannot therefore count on the absolute necessity of a black man voting Republican. . . .

Coming now to 1920 we have first to note that these experiences have not improved the temper of the Negro voter. In the first place, intelligence, not only as measured by formal schooling but as measured by wider social experience, is spreading fast in the Negro race and was quickened by the Great War. Black men are determined as never before not simply to vote but to make their votes tell. Intelligent leaders do not yet represent or control the majority of Negro voters, but this type of leadership is more widely effective today than ever before.

The calculations of the Republicans may first go awry in assuming that Negroes will not vote for Democrats. So far as the national Democratic ticket is concerned, this is of course perfectly true. No black man could vote for the "Solid South" and no Democratic candidate dare repudiate the support of this rotten borough system. But the Democratic organizations in certain northern states, and particularly in northern cities, have been giving a great deal of solicitous attention to Negroes. In New York City, for instance, there is a strong and intelligent Negro Democratic organization. The Negroes can get more consideration from the Democratic congressman in the one black Harlem district than from any of their Republican congressmen. They have consequently been voting more and more independently in Harlem in local elections and have their own representatives on the Board of Aldermen, in the Legislature, and in various branches of the civil service. In other cities and States the Democrats have made similar inroads.

It is quite possible, then, for Democratic congressmen, legislators, and governors to attract a considerable number of Negro votes and it is noticeable in this election that Negroes recognize that they are not nearly so much interested in the President of the United States as they are in their local aldermen and members of their state legislatures and particularly their congressmen.

Again the radicals have begun to see light with regard to Negroes. They realize that they must do more than flourish and beckon to get Negro support. The Committee of Forty-Eight has demanded: "equal economic, political and legal rights for all, irrespective of sex or color." The Socialist Party has put this plank in its platform: "Congress should enforce the provisions of the Fourteenth Amendment with reference to the Negroes, and effective Federal legislation should be enacted to secure to the Negroes full civil, political, industrial, and educational rights." The Labor Party has not been as explicit but it is making distinct overtures. Without doubt there will be a large Negro radical vote. . . .

What do Negroes expect to gain by political action? How far are they to be satisfied by platform dissertations on the Rights of Man? Do they expect to be legislated into complete modern freedom or have they thought out a clear straight political path leading to their ideals? Four years ago I could have answered these questions only by stating my own personal opinions. Today I can do more. The National Association for the Advancement of Colored People sent to seventeen presidential candidates and near candidates the following questionnaire:

1. Will you favor the enactment of laws making lynching a federal offense?
2. What is your attitude toward the disfranchisement of Americans of Negro descent: (a) will you advocate that Congress enforce the 14th Amendment and reduce the representation of states which disfranchise their citizens, or (b) will you advocate the appointment of United States Commissioners to enforce the 15th Amendment?
3. Will you endeavor to bring about the abolition of "Jim Crow" cars in interstate traffic?
4. Will you withdraw armed or other interference with the independence of Haiti?
5. Will you urge national aid to elementary education, without discrimination against Negro children?
6. Will you pledge the apportionment of Negro soldiers and Negro officers in the armed forces of the United States in proportion to their numbers in population?
7. Will you abolish racial segregation in the Civil Service of the United States?

Fifteen of those questioned preserved a discreet silence. Two replied but avoided committing themselves. Very well. The same or a similar questionnaire will go to every candidate for Congress. Some of these will refuse to answer while others like Dyer of Missouri and Madden of Illinois will hasten to answer favorably and in detail because a majority of their constituents are black and because, within the next four years, these men will be succeeded in Congress by black men. Other Negro congressmen loom in the far horizon in New York and Pennsylvania. The dilly-dallying of the Republicans has already beaten the Harlem districts of New York into the most independent voting district in the city. Party labels mean nothing there: A hundred thousand Negroes simply ask the candidates: Where do you stand on OUR problem?

This is symptomatic. The Republicans may ignore the Negro or pat him graciously on the back as in the past. The Democrats may continue to depend on oligarchy and mob rule in the South. Neither attitude will disturb the new Negro voter, for he expects it. He is simply going to seek to keep the Negro hater and the straddler out of Congress and the legislatures, and wherever possible he will support the candidate that stands for his Seven Points.

2 MARCUS GARVEY PREACHES BLACK PRIDE

A native of Jamaica, Marcus Garvey (1887–1940) founded his Universal Negro Improvement Association in 1914, and began its first chapter in the United States after he came to New York City in 1916. The movement flourished, especially among the Negro masses of the big cities, from whom men like DuBois and other NAACP leaders seemed so remote. Garvey preached that Negroes should be proud of all things black, and that they could find salvation only through a return to Africa. Arrested in 1923 for using the mails to defraud, Garvey was imprisoned in 1925, pardoned by President Coolidge in 1927, and then deported. By the mid-1920s his movement had begun to decline, but only after arousing the black masses to an extent never experienced before that time.

From Marcus Garvey, Philosophy and Opinions of Marcus Garvey, *ed. Amy Jacques-Garvey (New York: Universal Publishing House, 1925), 2: 37–41.*

Generally the public is kept misinformed of the truth surrounding new movements of reform. Very seldom, if ever, reformers get the truth told about them and their movements. Because of this natural attitude, the Universal Negro Improvement Association has been greatly handicapped in its work, causing thereby one of the most liberal and helpful human movements of the twentieth century to be held up to ridicule by those who take pride in poking fun at anything not already successfully established.

The white man of America has become the natural leader of the world. He, because of his exalted position, is called upon to help in all human efforts. From nations to individuals the appeal is made to him for aid in all things affecting humanity, so, naturally, there can be no great mass movement or change without first acquainting the leader on whose sympathy and advice the world moves.

It is because of this, and more so because of a desire to be Christian friends with the white race, why I explain the aims and objects of the Universal Negro Improvement Association.

The Universal Negro Improvement Association is an organization among Negroes that is seeking to improve the condition of the race, with the view of establishing a nation in Africa where Negroes will be given the opportunity to develop by themselves, without creating the hatred and animosity that now exist in countries of the white race through Negroes rivaling them for the highest and best positions in government, politics, society and industry. The organization believes in the rights of all men, yellow, white and black. To us, the white race has a right to the peaceful possession and occupation of countries of its own and in like manner the yellow and black races have their rights. It is only by an honest and liberal consideration of such rights can the world be blessed with the peace that is sought by Christian teachers and leaders.

THE SPIRITUAL BROTHERHOOD OF MAN

The following preamble to the constitution of the organization speaks for itself:

The Universal Negro Improvement Association and African Communities' League is a social, friendly, humanitarian, charitable, educational, institutional, constructive, and expansive society, and is founded by persons desiring to the utmost to work for the general uplift of the Negro peoples of the world. And the members pledge themselves to do all in their power to conserve the rights of their noble race and to respect the rights of all mankind, believing always in the Brotherhood of Man and the Fatherhood of God. The motto of the organization is: One God! One Aim! One Destiny! Therefore, let justice be done to all mankind, realizing that if the strong oppresses the weak confusion and discontent will ever mark the path of man, but with love, faith and charity toward all the reign of peace and plenty will be heralded into the world and the generation of men shall be called Blessed.

The declared objects of the association are:

To establish a Universal Confraternity among the race; to promote the spirit of pride and love; to reclaim the fallen; to administer to and assist the needy; to assist in civilizing the backward tribes of Africa; to assist in the development of Independent Negro Nations and Communities; to establish a central nation for the race; to establish Commissaries or Agencies in the principal countries and cities of the world for the representation of all Negroes; to promote a conscientious Spiritual worship among the native tribes of Africa; to establish Universities, Colleges, Academies and Schools for the racial education and culture of the people; to work for better conditions among Negroes everywhere.

SUPPLYING A LONG-FELT WANT

The organization of the Universal Negro Improvement Association has supplied among Negroes a long-felt want. Hitherto the other Negro movements in America, with the exception of the Tuskegee effort of Booker T. Washington, sought to teach the Negro to aspire to social equality with the whites, meaning thereby the right to intermarry and fraternize in every social way. This has been the source of much trouble and still some Negro organizations continue to preach this dangerous "race destroying doctrine" added to a program of political agitation and aggression. The Universal Negro Improvement Association on the other hand believes in and teaches the pride and purity of race. We believe that the white race should uphold its racial pride and perpetuate itself, and that the black race should do likewise. We believe that there is room enough in the world for the various race groups to grow and develop by themselves without seeking to destroy the Creator's plan by the constant introduction of mongrel types.

The unfortunate condition of slavery, as imposed upon the Negro, and which caused the mongrelization of the race, should not be legalized and continued now to the harm and detriment of both races.

The time has really come to give the Negro a chance to develop himself to a moral-standard man, and it is for such an opportunity that the Universal Negro Improvement Association seeks in the creation of an African nation for Negroes, where the greatest latitude would be given to work out this racial ideal.

There are hundreds of thousands of colored people in America who desire race amalgamation and miscegenation as a solution of the race problem. These people are, therefore, opposed to the race pride ideas of black and white; but the thoughtful of both races will naturally ignore the ravings of such persons and honestly work for the solution of a problem that has been forced upon us.

Liberal white America and race loving Negroes are bound to think at this time and thus evolve a program or plan by which there can be a fair and amicable settlement of the question.

We cannot put off the consideration of the matter, for time is pressing on our hands. The educated Negro is making rightful constitutional demands. The great white majority will never grant them, and thus we march on to danger if we do not now stop and adjust the matter.

The time is opportune to regulate the relationship between both races. Let the Negro have a country of his own. Help him to return to his original home, Africa, and there give him the opportunity to climb from the lowest to the highest positions in a state of his own. If not, then the nation will have to hearken to the demand of the aggressive, "social equality" organization, known as the National Association for the Advancement of Colored People, of which W. E. B. DuBois is leader, which declares vehemently for social and political equality, viz.: Negroes and whites in the same hotels, homes, residential districts, public and private places, a Negro as president, members of the Cabinet, Governors of States, Mayors of cities, and leaders of society in the United States. In this agitation, DuBois is ably supported by the "Chicago Defender," a colored newspaper published in Chicago. This paper advocates Negroes in the Cabinet and Senate. All these, as everybody knows, are the Negroes' constitutional rights, but reason dictates that the masses of the white race will never stand by the ascendency of an opposite minority group to the favored positions in a government, society and industry that exist by the will of the majority; hence the demand of the DuBois group of colored leaders will only lead, ultimately, to further disturbances in riots, lynching and mob rule. The only logical solution, therefore, is to supply the Negro with opportunities and environments of his own, and there point him to the fullness of his ambition.

NEGROES WHO SEEK SOCIAL EQUALITY

The Negro who seeks the White House in America could find ample play for his ambition in Africa. The Negro who seeks the office of Secretary of State in America would have a fair chance of demonstrating his diplomacy in Africa. The Negro who seeks a seat in the Senate or of being governor of a State in America, would be provided with a glorious chance for statesmanship in Africa.

The Negro has a claim on American white sympathy that cannot be denied. The Negro has labored for 300 years in contributing to America's greatness. White America will not be unmindful, therefore, of this consideration, but will treat him kindly. Yet it is realized that all human beings have a limit to their humanity. The humanity of white America, we realize, will seek self-protection and self-preservation, and that is why the thoughtful and reasonable Negro sees no hope in America for satisfying the aggressive program of the National Association for the Advancement of Colored People, but advances the reasonable plan of the Universal Negro Improvement Association, that of creating in Africa a nation and government for the Negro race.

This plan when properly undertaken and prosecuted will solve the race problem in America in fifty years. Africa affords a wonderful opportunity at the present time for colonization by the Negroes of the Western world. There is Liberia, already established as an independent Negro government. Let white America assist Afro-Americans to go there and help develop the country. Then, there are the late German colonies; let white sentiment force England and France to turn them over to the American and West Indian Negroes who fought for the Allies in the World War. Then, France, England and Belgium owe America billions of dollars which they claim they cannot afford to repay immediately. Let them compromise by turning over Sierra Leone and the Ivory Coast on the West Coast of Africa and add them to Liberia and help make Liberia a state worthy of her history.

The Negroes of Africa and America are one in blood. They have sprung from the same common stock. They can work and live together and thus make their own racial contribution to the world.

Will deep thinking and liberal white America help? It is a considerate duty.

It is true that a large number of self-seeking colored agitators and so-called political leaders, who hanker after social equality and fight for the impossible in politics and governments, will rave, but remember that the slave-holder raved, but the North said, "Let the slaves go free"; the British Parliament raved when the Colonists said, "We want a free and American nation"; the Monarchists of France raved when the people declared for a more liberal form of government.

The masses of Negroes think differently from the self-appointed leaders of the race. The majority of Negro leaders are selfish, self-appointed and not elected by the people. The people desire freedom in a land of their own, while the colored politician desires office and social equality for himself in America, and that is why we are asking white America to help the masses to realize their objective.

3   THE POLITICAL STATUS OF THE NORTHERN NEGRO IN 1941

*Despite their disillusionment with the Republican Party, in the absence
of a meaningful alternative, the great majority of black voters
continued to support the G.O.P. until the 1930s. But during the Great
Depression the myth of Lincoln proved to be an inadequate competitor
for the New Deal, and by 1936 a historic shift to the Democratic
Party of Franklin D. Roosevelt had been made. That decade also saw
the increased participation of Negroes in politics, at least in the North,
a fact that strengthened the hope that substantial improvements could
be made through proper use of the ballot. One of the most knowledgeable
students of the Negro's role in politics at that time was Dr. Ralph J.
Bunche, author of extensive research memoranda on the subject prepared
for Gunnar Myrdal's monumental work,* An American Dilemma.
*In this selection, written in 1941, Bunche assesses recent political
developments.*

*From Ralph J. Bunche, "The Negro in the Political Life of the
United States,"* The Journal of Negro Education *10 (July, 1941):
579–81. Reprinted by permission of The Bureau of Educational
Research, Howard University, and Ralph J. Bunche.*

Negro political activity in the North ties up importantly with the Negro
migrations during and after World War I. It was these migrations which
brought on the concentrations of Negro population in the Northern urban
centers. An outstanding characteristic of these new Negro populations,
which found themselves in a strange environment in the North, was their
political innocence. Inevitably, they fell prey to the machine politics of
the well-oiled political rings typical of America's great urban centers. An
essential corollary of the Negro's exploitation by political machines is the
frequent tie-up between Negro politics and politicians and the underworld.
For the most part this underworld association reduces itself to the numbers
and policy rackets and their numerous barons, to prostitution, and to
petty vice.

The Negro population of the North has adjusted itself rapidly to the political customs of its new environment. Negro voting behavior in the North today approximates the average. Negro participation at first was timid and meager; today it approaches the average. Negro party affiliation, which was once inflexibly Republican, today is no longer so; nor is the Negro's behavior longer atypical with regard to third-party support. Negro voting behavior in the North can no longer be described as generally atypical. The fact is that the Negro voter in the North is much more thoroughly assimilated politically than he is socially or economically. The Negro voter, like the white, is preyed upon by the political machines. The Negro voter, through his political leaders, who are professional politicians and therefore largely self-seeking, expects a direct return for his vote in the form of jobs, social and municipal services. Whereas in Chicago, New York, Cleveland, Philadelphia, St. Louis and Detroit, his vote is an important factor in determining election results, he does get improved facilities and services, though seldom in proportion to the real importance of his vote. Yet his vote, especially when political lieutenants can control it, is a voice that can command attention, and gives to the Negro of the North an effective lever that is almost entirely foreign to his black brother in the South.

The concentration of the Northern Negro in segregated residential areas has made for a more effective Negro vote. The Negro vote thus often controls the selection of local and state officials. Dividends in the form of local, state and federal patronage are now paid to the Negro as a matter of course. In numerous local elections the Negro vote has constituted the balance of power. In close national elections such as the last one, when the independent vote is considered a serious factor, the major parties carefully woo the Negro voters. The Negro vote is a constant threat and Negro organizations, such as the N.A.A.C.P., have made effective use of this threat in their lobbying activities on behalf of the Negro, notably in the successful fight against the confirmation of Judge Parker, and in the less-successful efforts in behalf of the anti-lynching bills.

There is really no accurate estimate of Negro voting in the North. The figure usually cited during the last presidential campaign exceeded 2,000,000. The claim is frequently made that the Negro controls the political balance of power in some seventeen of the Northern states. For the most part such "estimates" are mere guesses, based only upon the ratio of adult Negroes to the total adult population of the particular city or state. The Negro vote, moreover, is no longer a merely black vote, responsive only to racial appeals. Since 1928, when President Hoover pressed the Republican lily-white campaign in the South too overtly, and because the New Deal launched the relief and "forgotten man" appeals during the depression, there has been a decided shift in the political allegiance of the Northern Negro. The spell of the Lincoln legend over the Negro has been broken. It may well be, as some contend, that among well-to-do

Negroes it is still fashionable to be Republican, but it is also true that the working class, the unionized and the underprivileged Negro gives enthusiastic support to the Democratic party.

It is difficult to assess the real benefits accruing to the Northern Negro from his growing political activity. Prior to 1932, the great concentration on presidential campaigns paid only small dividends to the Negro masses, though Negro political leaders often plucked juicy patronage plums for themselves. But the New Deal for the first time gave broad recognition to the existence of the Negro as a national problem and undertook to give specific consideration to this fact in many ways, though the basic evils remain untouched.

The more immediate gains from political activity have resulted from the strategic rôle played by the Negro electorate in municipal campaigns. Here the Negro of the Northern cities has been able to trade his vote for tangible results—better schools, playground facilities, sanitation improvements, hospital accommodations, police and fire protection, transportation services, improved lighting and paving, municipal employment and office holding and direct representation. Though it can never be said that the Negro sections in general receive an equitable share of such benefits, it is undoubted that the conditions in the Negro residential areas of every Northern city in which the Negro wields a significant vote, would be much more neglected were it not for the power of that vote. The Negro is rapidly learning that he can trade and make demands upon the strength of his ballot.

The question is often raised as to whether the Negro vote is or should be a solid bloc vote. It is not so now, and even assuming that it were possible to make it so, this would be undesirable. The Negro population is properly subject to the same variations in interest as the white—there are sectional, class, religious, and ideological differences dividing the Negro vote as they divide the white. There is, for example, neither more nor less unanimity among Negroes with regards to the nation's foreign policy today than among whites. It is important to the proper functioning of democracy that this independence of attitude be preserved for all groups, granted the vital importance of national unity in this period of desperate crisis. While it is true that the Negro voter must always be a "race conscious" voter so long as racial division remains typical of American life, it is also true that there are many issues of even more fundamental importance than race to the welfare of the Negro voter here—not the least of which are those of broad governmental policy in the present crisis.

The Negro in the North experiences something of the real nature of political democracy. He has a political voice, a medium whereby he can express his views on and influence the direction of governmental policy. He has a hand in the selection of those who represent him in government. He is enabled, thereby, to develop a sense of responsibility and a feeling of dignity in a society in which he is permitted active participation. As an individual and as a group the Negro has a new, albeit proper, importance.

4 CONGRESSMAN ADAM CLAYTON POWELL

The first Negro to be elected to Congress in the twentieth century was Oscar DePriest of Chicago, who won his seat in 1928. Despite its large black population, New York City did not elect a Negro Congressman until 1944, a delay that can be explained in part by the fact that until district lines were redrawn the Negro vote had been split and rendered less effective. The new Representative was Adam Clayton Powell, one of the most colorful and controversial Negro leaders of his time. The following selection analyzes his career.

From James Q. Wilson, "The Flamboyant Mr. Powell," Commentary 41, No. 1 (January, 1966): 31–35. Reprinted by permission of Commentary and the author. Copyright © 1966 by the American Jewish Committee.

"Beware," Adam Clayton Powell once wrote, "of Greeks bearing gifts, colored men looking for loans, and whites who understand the Negro." He might well have excepted from this caution whites who "understand" Adam Powell, because most whites who think they understand him usually deplore him, and the more they deplore him the bigger the vote he amasses. Powell has been running against his real and imaginary white enemies for years and although he can now be re-elected to Congress without even the pretense of a campaign, he probably would like to have a few white critics on tap, just in case. . . .

The truth is that people are upset by Powell *because he is a Negro*, believing implicitly that Negroes, in this day and age, ought to produce selfless, honest, and dedicated leaders who will advance (genteelly) the cause of civil rights and Negro betterment. Powell knows this and capitalizes on it, though he gives it a quite different meaning. When his tax returns were investigated, when a grand jury was considering indicting him for taking kickbacks on the salary of a nominal secretary, when he went on trial for tax fraud, when he was condemned for junketing about Europe in lavish style, when an attempt was made to "purge" him in the

1958 Democratic primary, when he was convicted of libel—in all these cases and more, Powell's stock defense (and for his constituents, an effective one) was to charge that he was being "persecuted" because he was a Negro. That was never true in the sense in which he meant it. *Anti*-Negro feeling rarely, if ever, was at the source of his troubles; rather, it was *pro*-Negro feeling: the feeling that Powell should be better simply because the Negro cause deserves better.

While Powell was under attack by Senator John J. Williams (Rep., Delaware) for his European excursion and his curious financial transactions, a reporter asked him if Negro leaders shouldn't "lean over backwards" to avoid this sort of criticism. "I take the view," replied the Congressman, "that equality is equality . . . and that I am a member of Congress as good as anyone else. As long as it's within the law, it's not wrong." Later he added, "I do not do any more than any other member of the Congress, but by the Grace of God [*sic!*], I'll not do less!"

The real tragedy of Powell, and of Harlem's Negroes, is not that he should be a rogue (before the Great Society arrives and ennobles us all, there will be many more, black and white), but that he seems unable or unwilling to use the power that his style has produced for community or racial ends. . . .

. . . That Powell produces so little—that he is not likely to leave any monuments to himself, other than his church (and that he inherited from his father)—is in part due to the fact that his political base is a ghetto which cannot, unless led with great skill and cunning, provide a politician with ready-made power. J. Raymond Jones, the leader of what is left of Tammany Hall and a Negro of great political finesse, has come about as close as one could to translating Harlem votes into city-wide power. But he chose a very different route from Powell's and he chose it because, unlike Powell, he enjoys and wants power rather than headlines, the soft life, glamorous women, and villas in Puerto Rico.

The ghetto made Powell and the ghetto confines him, politically if not personally. But when power is placed in his hands, ready for use, he shows considerable skill at using it. Even many of his critics must admit that he has been a shrewd chairman of the House Committee on Education and Labor: he dominates it, directs it, and bargains with its power to get (among other things) what he feels are desirable changes in legislation concerning education, anti-poverty programs, job discrimination, and labor relations.

Powell prospers in chaos, when the organizationally-minded are distraught and at cross-purposes. The political chaos of Harlem in the 1930's gave Powell an opportunity to enter politics at the top, as a non-partisan, using his church as a base and a platform. Powell cannot, of course, be wholly "explained" by pointing out, correctly, that he was a maverick who entered a political vacuum caused by the decay of the party structure of Harlem in particular and Manhattan in general. Equally important was his unique personality and his position in a large and well-known church. It is just possible that, had there been a well-organized party system, Powell would have found a way to become its candidate. But it is not likely (flamboyant preachers who were openly flirting with the Communist party were not exactly the sort of person Tammany Hall was keenest on recruiting); in any case, if he had become a party man, his ambition and intelligence would surely have led him to trim his style to conform more nearly to the dictates of party regularity.

In 1938, scarcely one year after Powell succeeded his father as minister of the Abyssinian Baptist Church, he and a group of Harlem radicals formed the Greater New York Coordinating Committee for Unemployment (a vice-presidential candidate of the Communist party was on the committee; so were Negro ministers, writers, socialites, and some of the old cadres of the then-defunct Universal Negro Improvement Association of Marcus Garvey). Immediately it launched a boycott campaign against white merchants in Harlem, especially along 125th Street. "Don't buy where you can't work" was their slogan, as it was the slogan of similar groups in many Northern cities. The tactics which, twenty-five years later, were to be revived by civil-rights organizations, were pioneered in Harlem, though with a good deal less attention to the virtues of non-violence. Concessions were wrung from Consolidated Edison, the Telephone Company, small merchants, and the New York World's Fair. A bus boycott, aimed at getting Negroes hired as drivers and mechanics, was successful. Powell early displayed his mastery of the thinly-veiled threat: "Don't be hard on any Negroes you see on the buses this week," he suggested. "By next Monday if there are still people who have not seen the light yet, then convert them—one way or another." Martin Luther King would not have approved.

With the beginning of World War II, the Coordinating Committee floundered; out of it, Powell created the "People's Committee" for the purpose of getting him elected to the New York City Council. New York was governed by Fiorello LaGuardia (whom Powell detested—he once called for his impeachment) and reform was in fashion. The old Board of Aldermen, chosen by districts, had been abolished in 1937 and a new City Council, chosen at large by proportional representation, had been created. Under the old system, a short-sighted Tammany organization had drawn district lines and manipulated patronage to insure that no Negro would be elected; the new system, created to weaken further an already tottering Manhattan party organization, almost guaranteed that at least one Negro would be elected and in a way that would place a premium on personal publicity and freedom from party control. The expectations were fulfilled:

Powell was elected in 1941 (the first Negro to serve on the Council); when he decided in 1943 to leave the Council and run for Congress, he referred to the Negro Communist, Benjamin Davis, as "my logical successor." . . .

When he first sought office, Powell was endorsed by many of the good-government forces that had backed the new city charter, including . . . the CIO Trade Union Council, the United City Party, and others. Powell, like Curley, began as a "reformer." By the time the parties got around to dealing seriously with Harlem, Powell was in command and could not be dislodged. And by the time the good-government forces realized what their assault on the party system had produced as an alternative, Powell was immune to their criticisms. In 1944, he was elected to Congress from the newly-created all-Negro 22nd Congressional District; in the primary he won the nomination of the Democratic, Republican, and American Labor parties. . . .

Powell wasted no time in confirming the worst fears of those who viewed his rise to power with misgivings. He attacked President Truman as "The Little Man in the White House" (Powell had wanted Henry Wallace to be Roosevelt's vice-president in 1944). And when Mrs. Truman failed to heed a Powell demand that she not appear at a tea with leaders of the Daughters of the American Revolution (the DAR had refused to let Powell's wife, the pianist Hazel Scott, play in Constitution Hall), Powell called her the "Last Lady" and compared her unfavorably with Mrs. Eleanor Roosevelt, who had resigned from the DAR in 1939 in protest against Marian Anderson's exclusion from the same auditorium. Throughout the late 1940's and the 1950's, Powell enraged serious liberals by his repeated attempts to attach the so-called "Powell Amendment" to various bills providing federal aid to schools and other community facilities. The amendment would have barred the use of federal funds in segregated institutions; the liberals favored it in principle but felt that, under the circumstances, pushing it would only jeopardize already precarious liberal legislation. (By 1964, of course, the Powell Amendment had, in effect, become the law of the land through Title VI of the Civil Rights Act. Powell had little to do with that legislation.)

Powell was not the only maverick to serve Harlem in Congress. Vito Marcantonio was another Congressman who had defied the regular party machinery and won, in part on the strength of his considerable oratorical abilities, but the contrast between the two could not have been greater. Marcantonio used demagoguery to gain power which he then solidified by working intensively to build a vast network for dispensing social services and personal favors. Marcantonio loved power, and worked assiduously at creating it among the voters of East Harlem. Powell may have loved power, but he loved other things more—publicity, and the creature comforts. It would have been unthinkable, for example, for him to spend hot summer nights in a dingy Harlem office dealing with the myriad complaints of his constituents. To some extent, of course, Powell has used his church for that purpose, adding social and educational programs to its religious function. But Powell rarely participates personally in these programs; they have been run by hired professionals (sometimes with money he got from Washington) and church volunteers. For Powell, such an institution has been more a source of patronage with which he could take care of his lieutenants than a way of building up a network of reciprocal obligations among his voters. . . .

Harlem Negroes are fully aware that Powell uses community programs for personal ends. The *Amsterdam News* has consistently criticized him; so did Earl Brown, long before he allowed himself to be talked into being the candidate in the disastrous Tammany effort to "purge" Powell in the 1958 primary. Civil-rights leaders—A. Phillip Randolph, Roy Wilkins, Lester Granger, Whitney Young, Martin Luther King—have all harbored, both publicly and privately, well-known misgivings about the Congressman. And a 1964 New York *Times* poll in Harlem found that King was the overwhelming choice of Negroes as the leader who has done the most for them (King got 73 per cent of the votes, Powell only 21 per cent). Incredibly, many whites persist in thinking that this dissension means that Powell is weak or vulnerable and can thus be attacked. The point is, though, that any attack on Powell from a white person eliminates the dissension immediately, even if the attack is based on actions of his which seem to demonstrate his lack of concern for the Negro masses.

Anti-Negro whites have delighted in the way Powell conforms so abundantly to their stereotypes of the Negro—as a devotee of conspicuous consumption, as sexually profligate, as untrustworthy. Pro-Negro whites on the other hand have not been able to understand why Negro political leaders could not be more responsible, more committed, more constructive. Between Powell and William Dawson of Chicago, whose style is that of the quiet party regular, they find little to choose. Dawson they reject because of his seeming indifference in race matters (he is, to some, an "Uncle Tom"); and Powell they reject because his interest in race is "irresponsible." The assumption apparently has been that, during the 1940's and 1950's, the Negroes had the resources to produce something better. But that is far from clear. They lacked a large middle class; and they lacked in particular a commercial and entrepreneurial middle class which could provide the sort of civil infrastructure out of which might arise civic leaders, statesmen, and "good" politicians. And, above all, they had to win access to political power by taking it from whites not eager to surrender it. In these struggles, they perforce had to use the tools at hand, and these were primarily tools that the whites had fashioned.

Finally, a responsible agitation over race issues is not easily carried on within American electoral politics; in almost every case, changes have come—necessarily, it would seem—from institutions and forces outside the system: the courts, civil-rights organizations, and the changing temper of American public opinion. Partisan politics outside the South places a high premium on excluding fundamentally divisive issues from public debate; for most Negro politicians, as well as for most Northern white ones, the constraint operates effectively. When race is brought into politics by a man like Powell, it almost inevitably becomes distorted because the use of race as an issue is, in the first place, a reaction to a distorted political situation.

All this is changing. A new wave of reform is upon us, as evidenced by the sweeping reapportionment decisions, the renewed interest (in New York City, of all places!) in proportional representation, the reorganization of local government, the continued weakening of political parties, the rise to influence of new forces (especially the civil-rights groups), and the continued demand of the American public for "something better" by way of politics and politicians. And the Negro is changing—there is a larger and more affluent middle class, an increasingly restless lower class with a keener sense of relative deprivation, and a greater diversity of organizations and leaders. New kinds of Negro politicians will arise, but what kinds no one can predict. One thing seems clear: more Negro communities are becoming politically as volatile as Harlem in the 1930's, and thus the new politicians will all have, to some degree, a bit of Adam in them.

5   MARTIN LUTHER KING DESCRIBES MONTGOMERY'S MOMENT IN HISTORY

Legal action, a principal weapon of the civil rights movement of the 1940s and 1950s, achieved its greatest success with the case of Brown v. Board of Education of Topeka in May, 1954, when a unanimous Supreme Court held that state-enforced school segregation was an unconstitutional violation of the equal protection clause of the Fourteenth Amendment. Within a few years the courts had used similar reasoning in numerous other rulings to undermine the constitutional basis for racial segregation by state law in all public facilities. But the desegregation effort met determined southern resistance, and civil rights leaders found that in order to achieve their goals some sort of direct action in addition to litigation was

*necessary. The first big instance of this, and the one that most
caught the imagination of the country, was the Montgomery, Alabama,
bus boycott that began in December, 1955, and lasted for one year
until, assisted by a favorable Supreme Court ruling, bus desegregation
was finally achieved. The head of the Montgomery Improvement
Association, the Reverend Martin Luther King, Jr., emerged as the
most dynamic new leader of his race and the outstanding exponent
of the philosophy of nonviolent direct action. The decision for the
boycott is explained by Dr. King in this selection.*

From Martin Luther King, Jr., Stride Toward Freedom: The
Montgomery Story (*New York: Harper & Row, Publishers,
1958*), *pp. 43–45, 49–52, 64, 69–70. Copyright © 1958 by Martin
Luther King, Jr. Reprinted by permission of Harper & Row,
Publishers.*

On December 1, 1955, an attractive Negro seamstress, Mrs. Rosa
Parks, boarded the Cleveland Avenue Bus in downtown Montgomery.
She was returning home after her regular day's work in the Montgomery
Fair—a leading department store. Tired from long hours on her feet, Mrs.
Parks sat down in the first seat behind the section reserved for whites. Not
long after she took her seat, the bus operator ordered her, along with three
other Negro passengers, to move back in order to accommodate boarding
white passengers. By this time every seat in the bus was taken. This meant
that if Mrs. Parks followed the driver's command she would have to
stand while a white male passenger, who had just boarded the bus, would
sit. The other three Negro passengers immediately complied with the
driver's request. But Mrs. Parks quietly refused. The result was her arrest.

There was to be much speculation about why Mrs. Parks did not obey
the driver. Many people in the white community argued that she had been
"planted" by the NAACP in order to lay the groundwork for a test case,
and at first glance that explanation seemed plausible, since she was a
former secretary of the local branch of the NAACP. So persistent and
persuasive was this argument that it convinced many reporters from all
over the country. Later on, when I was having press conferences three
times a week—in order to accommodate the reporters and journalists who
came to Montgomery from all over the world—the invariable first question was: "Did the NAACP start the bus boycott?"

But the accusation was totally unwarranted, as the testimony of both
Mrs. Parks and the officials of the NAACP revealed. Actually, no one can
understand the action of Mrs. Parks unless he realizes that eventually the
cup of endurance runs over, and the human personality cries out, "I can
take it no longer." Mrs. Parks's refusal to move back was her intrepid

affirmation that she had had enough. It was an individual expression of a timeless longing for human dignity and freedom. She was not "planted" there by the NAACP, or any other organization; she was planted there by her personal sense of dignity and self-respect. She was anchored to that seat by the accumulated indignities of days gone by and the boundless aspirations of generations yet unborn. She was a victim of both the forces of history and the forces of destiny. She had been tracked down by the *Zeitgeist*—the spirit of the time.

Fortunately, Mrs. Parks was ideal for the role assigned to her by history. She was a charming person with a radiant personality, soft spoken and calm in all situations. Her character was impeccable and her dedication deep-rooted. All of these traits together made her one of the most respected people in the Negro community.

Only E. D. Nixon—the signer of Mrs. Parks's bond—and one or two other persons were aware of the arrest when it occurred early Thursday evening. Later in the evening the word got around to a few influential women of the community, mostly members of the Women's Political Council. After a series of telephone calls back and forth they agreed that the Negroes should boycott the buses. They immediately suggested the idea to Nixon, and he readily concurred. In his usual courageous manner he agreed to spearhead the idea.

Early Friday morning, December 2, Nixon called me. He was so caught up in what he was about to say that he forgot to greet me with the usual "hello" but plunged immediately into the story of what had happened to Mrs. Parks the night before. I listened, deeply shocked, as he described the humiliating incident. "We have taken this type of thing too long already," Nixon concluded, his voice trembling. "I feel that the time has come to boycott the buses. Only through a boycott can we make it clear to the white folks that we will not accept this type of treatment any longer."

I agreed at once that some protest was necessary, and that the boycott method would be an effective one. . . .

After a heavy day of work, I went home late Sunday afternoon and sat down to read the morning paper. There was a long article on the proposed boycott. Implicit throughout the article, I noticed, was the idea that the Negroes were preparing to use the same approach to their problem as the White Citizens Councils used. This suggested parallel had serious implications. The White Citizens Councils, which had had their birth in Mississippi a few months after the Supreme Court's school decision, had come into being to preserve segregation. The Councils had multiplied rapidly throughout the South, purporting to achieve their ends by the legal maneuvers of "interposition" and "nullification." Unfortunately, however, the actions of some of these Councils extended far beyond the bounds of the law. Their methods were the methods of open and covert terror, brutal intimidation, and threats of starvation to Negro men, women, and children. They took open economic reprisals against whites who dared to protest their defiance of the law, and the aim of their boycotts was not merely to impress their victims but to destroy them if possible.

Disturbed by the fact that our pending action was being equated with the boycott methods of the White Citizens Councils, I was forced for the first time to think seriously on the nature of the boycott. Up to this time I had uncritically accepted this method as our best course of action. Now certain doubts began to bother me. Were we following an ethical course of action? Is the boycott method basically unchristian? Isn't it a negative approach to the solution of a problem? Is it true that we would be following the course of some of the White Citizens Councils? Even if lasting practical results came from such a boycott, would immoral means justify moral ends? Each of these questions demanded honest answers.

I had to recognize that the boycott method could be used to unethical and unchristian ends. I had to concede, further, that this was the method used so often by the White Citizens Councils to deprive many Negroes, as well as white persons of good will, of the basic necessities of life. But certainly, I said to myself, our pending actions could not be interpreted in this light. Our purposes were altogether different. We would use this method to give birth to justice and freedom, and also to urge men to comply with the law of the land; the White Citizens Councils used it to perpetuate the reign of injustice and human servitude, and urged men to defy the law of the land. I reasoned, therefore, that the word "boycott" was really a misnomer for our proposed action. A boycott suggests an economic squeeze, leaving one bogged down in a negative. But we were concerned with the positive. Our concern would not be to put the bus company out of business, but to put justice in business.

As I thought further I came to see that what we were really doing was withdrawing our cooperation from an evil system, rather than merely withdrawing our economic support from the bus company. The bus company, being an external expression of the system, would naturally suffer, but the basic aim was to refuse to cooperate with evil. At this point I began to think about Thoreau's *Essay on Civil Disobedience*. I remembered how, as a college student, I had been moved when I first read this work. I became convinced that what we were preparing to do in Montgomery was related to what Thoreau had expressed. We were simply saying to the white community, "We can no longer lend our cooperation to an evil system."

Something began to say to me, "He who passively accepts evil is as much involved in it as he who helps to perpetrate it. He who accepts evil without protesting against it is really cooperating with it." When oppressed people willingly accept their oppression they only serve to give the oppressor a convenient justification for his acts. Often the oppressor goes along unaware of the evil involved in his oppression so long as the oppressed accepts it. So in order to be true to one's conscience and true to God, a righteous man has no alternative but to refuse to cooperate with an evil system. This I felt was the nature of our action. From this moment on I conceived of our movement as an act of massive noncooperation. From then on I rarely used the word "boycott." . . .

Many will inevitably raise the question, why did this event take place in Montgomery, Alabama, in 1955? Some have suggested that the Supreme Court decision on school desegregation, handed down less than two years before, had given new hope of eventual justice to Negroes everywhere, and fired them with the necessary spark of encouragement to rise against their oppression. But although this might help to explain why the protest occurred when it did, it cannot explain why it happened in Montgomery.

Certainly, there is a partial explanation in the long history of injustice on the buses of Montgomery. The bus protest did not spring into being full grown as Athena sprang from the head of Zeus; it was the culmination of a slowly developing process. Mrs. Parks's arrest was the precipitating factor rather than the cause of the protest. The cause lay deep in the record of similar injustices. Almost everybody could point to an unfortunate episode that he himself had experienced or seen.

But there comes a time when people get tired of being trampled by oppression. There comes a time when people get tired of being plunged into the abyss of exploitation and nagging injustice. The story of Montgomery is the story of 50,000 such Negroes who were willing to substitute tired feet for tired souls, and walk the streets of Montgomery until the walls of segregation were finally battered by the forces of justice.

But neither is this the whole explanation. Negroes in other communities confronted conditions equally as bad, and often worse. So we cannot explain the Montgomery story merely in terms of the abuses that Negroes suffered there. Moreover, it cannot be explained by a preexistent unity among the leaders, since we have seen that the Montgomery Negro community prior to the protest was marked by divided leadership, indifference, and complacency. Nor can it be explained by the appearance upon the scene of new leadership. The Montgomery story would have taken place if the leaders of the protest had never been born.

So every rational explanation breaks down at some point. There is something about the protest that is suprarational; it cannot be explained without a divine dimension. Some may call it a principle of concretion, with Alfred N. Whitehead; or a process of integration, with Henry N. Wieman; or Being-itself, with Paul Tillich; or a personal God. Whatever the name, some extra-human force labors to create a harmony out of the discords of the universe. There is a creative power that works to pull down mountains of evil and level hilltops of injustice. God still works through history His wonders to perform. It seems as though God had decided to use Montgomery as the proving ground for the struggle and triumph of freedom and justice in America. And what better place for it than the leading symbol of the Old South? It is one of the splendid ironies of our day that Montgomery, the Cradle of the Confederacy, is being transformed into Montgomery, the cradle of freedom and justice.

The day of days, Monday, December 5, 1955, was drawing to a close. We all prepared to go to our homes, not yet fully aware of what had happened. The deliberations of that brisk, cool night in December will not be forgotten. That night we were starting a movement that would gain national recognition, whose echoes would ring in the ears of people of every nation, a movement that would astound the oppressor, and bring new hope to the oppressed. That night was Montgomery's moment in history.

6 CHARLES V. HAMILTON DEFINES BLACK POWER

During the latter half of the 1960s, the expression "black power" rapidly became a very popular rallying cry, and one that thoroughly frightened many whites. As some of the other selections in this book indicate, however, some of the ideas of black power, if not the exact terminology, had been expressed by Negro leaders at various times in the past. One of the most articulate recent advocates of black power is Charles V. Hamilton, a professor of political science at Columbia University, whose definition of the concept is reprinted here.

From Charles V. Hamilton, "An Advocate of Black Power Defines It," New York Times Magazine, *April 14, 1968, pp. 22–23, 79–83.* © *1968 by The New York Times Company. Reprinted by permission.*

Black power has many definitions and connotations in the rhetoric of race relations today. To some people, it is synonymous with premeditated acts of violence to destroy the political and economic institutions of this country. Others equate Black Power with plans to rid the civil-rights movement of whites who have been in it for years. The concept is understood by many to mean hatred of and separation from whites; it is associated with calling whites "honkies" and with shouts of "Burn, baby, burn!" Some understand it to be the use of pressure-group tactics in the accepted tradition of the American political process. And still others say that Black Power must be seen first of all as an attempt to instill a sense of identity and pride in black people.

Ultimately, I suspect, we have to accept the fact that, in this highly charged atmosphere, it is virtually impossible to come up with a single definition satisfactory to all.

Even as some of us try to articulate our idea of Black Power and the way we relate to it and advocate it, we are categorized as "moderate" or "militant" or "reasonable" or "extremist." "I can accept your definition of Black Power," a listener will say to me. "But how does your position compare with what Stokely Carmichael said in Cuba or with what H. Rap Brown said in Cambridge, Md.?" Or, just as frequently, some young white New Left advocate will come up to me and proudly announce: "You're not radical enough. Watts, Newark, Detroit—that's what's happening, man! You're nothing but a reformist. We've got to blow up this society. Read Ché or Debray or Mao." All I can do is shrug and conclude that some people believe that making a revolution in this country involves rhetoric, Molotov cocktails and being under 30.

To have Black Power equated with calculated acts of violence would be very unfortunate. First, if black people have learned anything over the years, it is that he who shouts revolution the loudest is one of the first to run when the action starts. Second, open calls to violence are a sure way to have one's ranks immediately infiltrated. Third—and this is as important as any reason—violent revolution in this country would fail; it would be met with the kind of repression used in Sharpeville, South Africa, in 1960, when 67 Africans were killed and 186 wounded during a demonstration against apartheid. It is clear that America is not above this. There are many white bigots who would like nothing better than to embark on a program of black genocide, even though the imposition of such repressive measures would destroy civil liberties for whites as well as for blacks. Some whites are so panicky, irrational and filled with racial hatred that they would welcome the opportunity to annihilate the black community. This was clearly shown in the senseless murder of Dr. Martin Luther King, Jr., which understandably—but nonetheless irrationally—prompted some black militants to advocate violent retaliation. Such cries for revenge intensify racial fear and animosity when the need—now more than ever—is to establish solid, stable organizations and action programs.

Many whites will take comfort in these words of caution against violence. But they should not. The truth is that the black ghettos are going to continue to blow up out of sheer frustration and rage, and no amount of rhetoric from professors writing articles in magazines (which most black people in the ghettos do not read anyway) will affect that. There comes a point beyond which people cannot be expected to endure prejudice, oppression and deprivation, and they *will* explode.

Some of us can protect our positions by calling for "law and order" during a riot, or by urging "peaceful" approaches, but we should not be confident that we are being listened to by black people legitimately fed up with intolerable conditions. If white America wants a solution to the violence in the ghettos by blacks, then let white America end the violence done to the ghettos by whites. We simply must come to understand that there can be no social order without social justice. "How long will the violence in the summers last?" another listener may ask. "How intransigent is white America?" is my answer. And the answer to that could be just more rhetoric or it could be a sincere response to legitimate demands.

Black power must not be naive about the intentions of white decision-makers to yield anything without a struggle and a confrontation by organized power. Black people will gain only as much as they can win through their ability to organize independent bases of economic and political power—through boycotts, electoral activity, rent strikes, work stoppages, pressure-group bargaining. And it must be clear that whites will have to bargain with blacks or continue to fight them in the streets of the Detroits and the Newarks. Rather than being a call to violence, this is a clear recognition that the ghetto rebellions, in addition to producing the possibility of apartheid-type repression, have been functional in moving *some* whites to see that viable solutions must be sought.

Black Power is concerned with organizing the rage of black people and with putting new, hard questions and demands to white America. As we do this, white America's responses will be crucial to the questions of violence and viability. Black Power must (1) deal with the obviously growing alienation of black people and their distrust of the institutions of this society; (2) work to create new values and to build a new sense of community and of belonging; and (3) work to establish legitimate new institutions that make participants, not recipients, out of a people traditionally excluded from the fundamentally racist processes of this country. There is nothing glamorous about this; it involves persistence and hard, tedious, day-to-day work.

Black Power rejects the lessons of slavery and segregation that caused black people to look upon themselves with hatred and disdain. To be "integrated" it was necessary to deny one's heritage, one's own culture, to be ashamed of one's black skin, thick lips and kinky hair. In their book, "Racial Crisis in America," two Florida State University sociologists, Lewis M. Killian and Charles M. Grigg, wrote: "At the present time, integration as a solution to the race problem demands that the Negro forswear his identity as a Negro. But for a lasting solution, the meaning of

'American' must lose its implicit racial modifier, 'white.' " The black man must change his demeaning conception of himself; he must develop a sense of pride and self-respect. Then, if integration comes, it will deal with people who are psychologically and mentally healthy, with people who have a sense of their history and of themselves as whole human beings.

In the process of creating these new values, Black Power will, its advocates hope, build a new sense of community among black people. It will try to forge a bond in the black community between those who have "made it" and those "on the bottom." It will bring an end to the internal back-biting and suspicious bickering, the squabbling over tactics and personalities so characteristic of the black community. If Black Power can produce this unity, that in itself will be revolutionary, for the black community and for the country.

Black Power recognizes that new forms of decision-making must be implemented in the black community. One purpose, clearly, is to overcome the alienation and distrust.

Let me deal with this specifically by looking at the situation in terms of "internal" and "external" ghetto problems and approaches. When I speak of internal problems, I refer to such things as exploitative merchants who invade the black communities, to absentee slumlords, to inferior schools and arbitrary law enforcement, to black people unable to develop their own independent economic and political bases. There are, of course, many problems facing black people which must be dealt with outside the ghettos: jobs, open occupancy, medical care, higher education.

The solution of the internal problems does not require the presence of massive numbers of whites marching arm in arm with blacks. Local all-black groups can organize boycotts of disreputable merchants and of those employers in the black communities who fail to hire and promote black people. Already, we see this approach spreading across the country with Operation Breadbasket, initiated by Dr. King's Southern Christian Leadership Conference. The national director of the program, the Rev. Jesse Jackson, who was with Dr. King when he was murdered in Memphis, has established several such projects from Los Angeles to Raleigh, N.C.

In Chicago alone, in 15 months, approximately 2,000 jobs worth more than $15 million in annual income were obtained for black people. Negotiations are conducted on hiring and upgrading black people, marketing the products of black manufacturers and suppliers and providing contracts to black companies. The operation relies heavily on the support of black businessmen, who are willing to work with Operation Breadbasket because it is mutually beneficial. They derive a profit and in turn contribute to the economic development of the black community.

This is Black Power in operation. But there is not nearly enough of this kind of work going on. In some instances, there is a lack of technical know-how coupled with a lack of adequate funds. These two defects constantly plague constructive pressure-group activity in the black communities. . . .

In New York, Black Power, in the way we see it, operates through a group called N.E.G.R.O. (National Economic Growth and Reconstruction Organization). Its acronym does not sit too well with some advocates of black consciousness who see in the use of the term "Negro" an indication of less than sufficient racial pride. Started in 1964, the group deals with economic self-help for the black community: a hospital in Queens, a chemical corporation, a textile company and a construction company. N.E.G.R.O., with an annual payroll of $1 million and assets of $3 million, is headed by Dr. Thomas W. Matthew, a neurosurgeon who has been accused of failing to file Federal income-tax returns for 1961, 1962 and 1963. He has asserted that he will pay all the Government says he owes, but not until "my patient is cured or one of us dies." His patient is the black community, and the emphasis of his group is on aiding blacks and reducing reliance on the white man. The organization creates a sense of identity and cohesiveness that is painfully lacking in much of the black community.

In helping oneself and one's race through hard work, N.E.G.R.O. would appear to be following the Puritan ethic of work and achievement: if you work hard, you will succeed. One gets the impression that the organization is not necessarily idealistic about this. It believes that black people will never develop in this country as long as they must depend on hand-outs from the white man. This is realism, whatever ethic it is identified with. And this, too, is Black Power in operation. . . .

Absolutely crucial to the development of Black Power is the black middle class. These are people with sorely needed skills. There has been a lot of discussion about where the black middle class stands in relation to Black Power. Some people adopt the view that most members of the class opt out of the race (or at least try to do so); they get good jobs, a nice home, two cars, and forget about the masses of blacks who have not "made it." This has been largely true. Many middle-class blacks simply do not feel an obligation to help the less fortunate members of their race.

There is, however, a growing awareness among black middle-class people of their role in the black revolution. On January 20, a small group of them (known, appropriately enough, as the Catalysts) called an all-day conference in a South Side Chicago church to discuss ways of linking black middle-class professionals with black people in the lower class. Present were about 370 people of all sorts: teachers, social workers, lawyers, accountants, three physicians, housewives, writers. They met in workshops to discuss ways of making their skills and positions relevant to the black

society, and they held no press conferences. Though programs of action
developed, the truth is that they remain the exception, not the rule, in the
black middle class.

Another group has been formed by black teachers in Chicago, Detroit
and New York, and plans are being made to expand. In Chicago, the
organization is called the Association of Afro-American Educators. These
are people who have traditionally been the strongest supporters of the
status quo. Education is intended to develop people who will support the
existing values of the society, and "Negro" teachers have been helping
this process over the years. But now some of them (more than 250 met on
February 12 in Chicago) are organizing and beginning to redefine, first,
their role as black educators vis-à-vis the black revolution, and, second,
the issues as they see them. Their motivation is outlined in the following
statement:

> By tapping our vast resources of black intellectual expertise, we shall gen-
> erate new ideas for *meaningful* educational programs, curricula and instructional
> materials which will contribute substantially toward raising the educational
> achievement of black children.
>
> Our purpose is to extricate ourselves momentarily from the dominant society
> in order to realign our priorities, to mobilize and to "get ourselves together"
> to do what must be done by those best equipped to do it.

This is what they say; whether they can pull it off will depend initially
on their ability to bring along their black colleagues, many of whom,
admittedly, do not see the efficacy of such an attitude. Unless the link is
made between the black middle-class professionals and the black masses,
Black Power will probably die on the speaker's platform.

Another important phenomenon in the development of Black Power is
the burgeoning of black students' groups on college campuses across the
country. I have visited 17 such campuses—from Harvard to Virginia to
Wisconsin to U.C.L.A.—since October. The students are discussing problems of identity, of relevant curricula at their universities, of ways of helping their people when they graduate. Clearly, one sees in these hundreds
(the figure could be in the thousands) of black students a little bit of Booker
T. Washington (self-help and the dignity of common labor) and a lot of
W. E. B. DuBois (vigorous insistence on equality and the liberal education
of the most talented black men).

These are the people who are planning to implement social, political
and economic Black Power in their home towns. They will run for public
office, aware that Richard Hatcher started from a political base in the
black community. He would not be Mayor of Gary, Indiana, today if he
had not first mobilized the black voters. Some people point out that he had
to have white support. This is true; in many instances such support is
necessary, but internal unity is necessary first.

This brings us to a consideration of the external problems of the black community. It is clear that black people will need the help of whites at many places along the line. There simply are not sufficient economic resources—actual or potential—in the black community for a total, unilateral, boot-strap operation. Why should there be? Black people have been the target of deliberate denial for centuries, and racist America has done its job well. This is a serious problem that must be faced by Black Power advocates. On the one hand, they recognize the need to be independent of "the white power structure." And on the other, they must frequently turn to that structure for help—technical and financial. Thus, the rhetoric and the reality often clash.

Resolution probably lies in the realization by white America that it is in her interest not to have a weak, dependent, alienated black community inhabiting the inner cities and blowing them up periodically. Society needs stability, and as long as there is a sizable powerless, restless group within it which considers the society illegitimate, stability is not possible. However it is calculated, the situation calls for a black-white rapprochement, which may well come only through additional confrontations and crises. More frequently than not, the self-interest of the dominant society is not clearly perceived until the brink is reached.

There are many ways whites can relate to this phenomenon. First, they must recognize that blacks are going to insist on an equitable distribution of *decision-making power*. Anything less will simply be perpetuating a welfare mentality among blacks. And if the society thinks only in terms of *giving* more jobs, better schools and more housing, the result will be the creation of more black recipients still dependent on whites.

The equitable distribution of power must result from a conviction that it is a matter of mutual self-interest, not from the feelings of guilt and altruism that were evident at the National Conference of New Politics convention in Chicago in August. An equitable distribution means that black men will have to occupy positions of political power in precincts, counties, Congressional districts and cities where their numbers and organization warrant. It means the end of absentee white ward committeemen and precinct captains in Chicago's black precincts.

But this situation is much easier described than achieved. Black Americans generally are no more likely to vote independently than other Americans. In many Northern urban areas, especially, the job of wooing the black vote away from the Democratic party is gigantic. The established machine has the resources: patronage, tradition, apathy. In some instances the change will take a catalytic event—a major racial incident, a dramatic black candidate, a serious boner by the white establishment (such as splitting the white vote). The mere call to "blackness" simply is not enough, even where the numbers are right.

In addition, many of the problems facing black people can be solved only to the extent that whites are willing to see such imperatives as an open housing market and an expanding job market. White groups must continue to bring as much pressure as possible on local and national decision-makers to adopt sound policy in these fields. These enlightened whites *will* be able to work with Black Power groups.

There are many things which flow from this orientation to Black Power. It is not necessary that blacks create parallel agencies—political or economic—in all fields and places. In some areas, it is possible to work within, say, the two-party system. Richard Hatcher did so in Gary, but he first had to organize black voters to fight the Democratic machine in the primary. The same is true of Mayor Carl Stokes in Cleveland. At some point it may be wise to work with the existing agencies, but this must be done only from a base of independent, not subordinated, power.

On the other hand, dealing with a racist organization like George Wallace's Democratic party in Alabama would require forming an independent group. The same is true with some labor unions, especially in the South, which still practice discrimination despite the condemnation of such a policy by their parent unions. Many union locals are willing to work with their black members on such matters as wages and working conditions, but refuse to join the fight for open housing laws.

The point is that black people must become much more pragmatic in their approach. Whether we try to work within or outside a particular agency should depend entirely on a hard-nosed, calculated examination of potential success in each situation—a careful analysis of cost and benefit. Thus, when we negotiate the test will be: How will black people, not some political machine downtown or some labor union boss across town, benefit from this?

Black Power must insist that the institutions in the black community be led by and, wherever possible, staffed by blacks. This is advisable psychologically, and it is necessary as a challenge to the myth that black people are incapable of leadership. Admittedly, this violates the principle of egalitarianism ("We hire on the basis of merit alone, not color"). What black and white America must understand is that egalitarianism is just a *principle* and it implies a notion of "color-blindness" which is deceptive. It must be clear by now that any society which has been color-conscious all its life to the detriment of a particular group cannot simply become color-blind and expect that group to compete on equal terms.

Black Power clearly recognizes the need to perpetuate color consciousness, but in a positive way—to improve a group, not to subject it. When principles like egalitarianism have been so flagrantly violated for so long, it does not make sense to think that the victim of that violation can be equipped to benefit from opportunities simply upon their pronouncement.

Obviously, some positive form of special treatment must be used to overcome centuries of negative special treatment.

This has been the argument of the Nation of Islam (the so-called Black Muslims) for years; it has also been the position of the National Urban League since its proposal for preferential treatment (the Domestic Marshall Plan, which urged a "special effort to overcome serious disabilities resulting from historic handicaps") was issued at its 1963 Denver convention. This is not racism. It is not intended to penalize or subordinate another group; its goal is the positive uplift of a deliberately repressed group. Thus, when some Black Power advocates call for the appointment of black people to head community-action poverty programs and to serve as school principals, they have in mind the deliberate projection of blacks into positions of leadership. This is important to give other black people a feeling of ability to achieve, if nothing else. And it is especially important for young black children.

An example of concentrated special treatment is the plan some of us are proposing for a new approach to education in some of the black ghettos. It goes beyond the decentralization plans in the Bundy Report; it goes beyond the community involvement at I.S. 201 in Harlem. It attempts to build on the idea proposed by Harlem CORE last year for an independent Board of Education for Harlem.

Harlem CORE and the New York Urban League saw the Bundy Report as a "step toward creating a structure which would bring meaningful education to the children of New York." CORE, led by Roy Innis, suggested an autonomous Harlem school system, chartered by the State Legislature and responsible to the state. "It will be run by an elected school board and an appointed administrator, as most school boards are," CORE said. "The elected members will be Harlem residents. It is important that much of the detailed planning and structure be the work of the Harlem community." Funds would come from city, state and Federal governments and from private sources. In describing the long-range goal of the proposal, CORE says: "Some have felt it is to create a permanently separate educational system. Others have felt it is a necessary step toward eventual integration. In any case, the ultimate outcome of this plan will be to make it possible for Harlem to choose." . . .

Black Power has been accused of emphasizing decentralization, of overlooking the obvious trend toward consolidation. This is not true with the kind of Black Power described here, which is ultimately not separatist or isolationist. Some Black Power advocates are aware that this country is simultaneously experiencing centralization and decentralization. As the Federal Government becomes more involved (and it must) in the lives of people, it is imperative that we broaden the base of citizen participation. It will be the new forms, new agencies and structures developed by Black Power that will link these centralizing and decentralizing trends.

Black Power structures at the local level will activate people, instill faith (not alienation) and provide a habit of organization and a consciousness of ability. Alienation will be overcome and trust in society restored. It will be through these local agencies that the centralized forces will operate, not through insensitive, unresponsive city halls. Billions of dollars will be needed each year, and these funds must be provided through a more direct route from their sources to the people.

Black Power is a developmental process; it cannot be an end in itself. To the extent that black Americans can organize, and to the extent that white Americans can keep from panicking and begin to respond rationally to the demands of that organization—to that extent can we get on with the protracted business of creating not just law and order but a free and open society.

For Additional Reading

The most useful general history of the Negro in America is still John Hope Franklin, *From Slavery to Freedom*, 3rd ed. (New York: Alfred A. Knopf, Inc., 1967). For an incisive shorter work, see August Meier and Elliott M. Rudwick, *From Plantation to Ghetto: An Interpretive History of American Negroes* (New York: Hill and Wang, Inc., 1966). Three excellent recent studies of the development of the black ghetto in two large northern cities are Gilbert Osofsky, *Harlem: The Making of a Ghetto* (New York: Harper & Row, Publishers, 1966); Seth M. Scheiner, *Negro Mecca: A History of the Negro in New York City, 1865–1920* (New York: New York University Press, 1965); and Allan H. Spear, *Black Chicago: The Making of a Negro Ghetto, 1890–1920* (Chicago: The University of Chicago Press, 1967). A valuable older work on Chicago is St. Clair Drake and Horace R. Cayton, *Black Metropolis: A Study of Negro Life in a Northern City*, revised and enlarged Torchbook ed., 2 vols. (New York: Harper & Row, Publishers, 1962). The history of the Negro in Washington, D.C., is traced in Constance McLaughlin Green, *The Secret City: A History of Race Relations in the Nation's Capital* (Princeton: Princeton University Press, 1967).

The urban migration is surveyed in Arna Bontemps and Jack Conroy, *Anyplace But Here* (New York: Hill and Wang, Inc., 1966). A recent systematic account of residential segregation is Karl E. Taeuber and Alma F. Taeuber, *Negroes in Cities: Residential Segregation and Neighborhood Change* (Chicago: Aldine Publishing Co., 1965). On the job situation through the World War II period, see Robert C. Weaver, *Negro Labor: A National Problem* (New York: Harcourt, Brace and Co., 1946). Louis Ruchames, *Race, Jobs, and Politics: The Story of FEPC* (New York: Columbia University Press, 1953), evaluates the federal government's effort to prevent job discrimination in defense industries.

The best introduction to the Harlem Renaissance is Alain Locke, ed., *The New*

Negro (New York: Albert and Charles Boni, 1925), while Langston Hughes, *The Big Sea* (New York: Alfred A. Knopf, Inc., 1940) is one of the most interesting accounts by a participant. Hughes's experience should be contrasted with the urban America portrayed in *The Autobiography of Malcolm X* (New York: Grove Press, Inc., 1963) and Claude Brown, *Manchild in the Promised Land* (New York: Macmillan Co., 1965). On Afro-American music, see LeRoi Jones, *Blues People: Negro Music in White America* (New York: William Morrow and Co., 1963). E. Franklin Frazier, *The Negro Church in America* (New York: Schocken Books, 1963) is a perceptive short analysis. Lee Rainwater and William L. Yancey, *The Moynihan Report and the Politics of Controversy* (Cambridge: The M.I.T. Press, 1967) brings together a wealth of critical material by many writers on the question of the Negro family. For another recent discussion see Andrew Billingsley, *Black Families in White America* (Englewood Cliffs, N.J.: Prentice-Hall, Inc., 1968).

The United States Commission on Civil Rights has published a number of reports on various aspects of the urban school crisis. See in particular its *Racial Isolation in the Public Schools* (Washington, D.C.: U.S. Government Printing Office, 1967). The most important and controversial recent study comparing black and white educational opportunities and accomplishments is James S. Coleman et al., *Equality of Educational Opportunity* (Washington, D.C.: U.S. Government Printing Office, 1966). Few writers have expressed the crushing effects of bad schools on ghetto children as poignantly as Jonathan Kozol, *Death At An Early Age* (Boston: Houghton Mifflin Co., 1967).

One of the worst riots of the World War I period is extensively analyzed in Elliott M. Rudwick, *Race Riot at East St. Louis, July 2, 1917* (Carbondale: Southern Illinois University Press, 1964). For a broader study of the problem of violence see Arthur I. Waskow, *From Race Riot to Sit-In, 1919 and the 1960's* (Garden City, New York: Doubleday and Co., 1966). The report of the 1965 Watts riot in Los Angeles prepared by the Governor's Commission headed by John A. McCone, *Violence in the City—An End or a Beginning?* (Los Angeles: Lucas Brother, Publishers, 1965), has been strongly attacked. See particularly Paul Jacobs, *Prelude to Riot: A View of Urban America From the Bottom* (New York: Random House, Inc., 1968).

Edmund David Cronon, *Black Moses: The Story of the Marcus Garvey and the Universal Negro Improvement Association* (Madison: University of Wisconsin Press, 1955) sympathetically describes the first really significant mass movement among American Negroes. The increased impact of the Negro on national politics is explored in Henry L. Moon, *Balance of Power: The Negro Vote* (Garden City, New York: Doubleday and Co., 1948). The amount of recent literature on civil rights and Negro protest movements is enormous and growing. For a statement by a moderate Negro leader see Whitney M. Young, Jr., *To Be Equal* (New York: McGraw-Hill Book Company, 1964). A somewhat different point of view is presented in Stokely Carmichael and Charles V. Hamilton, *Black Power: The Politics of Liberation in America* (New York: Random House, Inc., 1967).